But Now is Christ Risen From the Dead
—1 Corinthians 15:20

EVIDENCE
FOR THE
HISTORICAL JESUS

IS THE JESUS OF HISTORY THE
CHRIST OF FAITH?

GARY R. HABERMAS

EVIDENCE FOR THE HISTORICAL JESUS

Is the Jesus of History the Christ of Faith

Gary R. Habermas

Christian Publishing House

Cambridge, Ohio

EVIDENCE FOR THE HISTORICAL JESUS: Is the Jesus of History the Christ of Faith by Gary R. Habermas

ISBN-13: **978-1-949586-67-1**

ISBN-10: **1-949586-67-7**

This publication is an edited transcript from The John Ankerberg Show, 2000 (with permission). This edition is entirely reviewed and updated to June 2015 by Prof Gary Habermas.

Table of Contents

Introduction

The subject of the Historical Jesus is perhaps the most popular religious topic in settings such as university and seminary classrooms, written volumes, and doctoral dissertations. Unlike many of these more formal situations, the question-and-answer format utilized throughout this text allows plenty of space to develop additional angles. Hence, the backtracking, necessary repetition, as well as viewing the subject matter from a variety of perspectives, allow the conversation to deepen significantly before moving ahead. In the process, it is our hope that new ideas will be expressed and developed. The overall purpose is to provide a historical context for the original gospel proclamation as provided by Jesus' disciples at a very early date after the crucifixion itself. If we have come close to providing such a basis, then we will have reached our central goal.

This volume is a transcribed and expanded version of six television programs that appeared originally on "The John Ankerberg Show." The original material was used by permission, for which we begin by thanking Dr. John Ankerberg, Alan Weathers, and their associates. This explains the similar introduction which appears at the beginning of each program, which has been left out here to avoid redundancy, as well as extra costs to the reader.

PROGRAM 1 What Does Mainstream Scholarship Think about the Conclusions of the Jesus Seminar?

Introduction

Dr. John Ankerberg: The search for the historical Jesus is a hot topic in both popular and academic circles today and has drawn a lot of attention from national magazines, such as *Time*, *Newsweek*, and *U.S. News & World Report*. Further, the media has given an undue amount of attention to the outlandish statements of the Jesus Seminar, a self-selected liberal group representing a very small percentage of New Testament scholarship. Today we will address the questions surrounding the debate over the historical Jesus and show there are a significant number of historical facts about Jesus in secular and non-New Testament sources that prove that the Jesus of history is the same Jesus of the Christian faith.

My guest is world-class philosopher Dr. Gary Habermas, author of the book, *The Historical Jesus* and about twenty other volumes. He received his Ph.D. from Michigan State University. Dr. Habermas is chairman of the Department of Philosophy at Liberty University. He has written more than 100 articles, mostly on the life of Jesus, which have appeared in scholarly journals and elsewhere. Join us for this edition of The John Ankerberg Show and learn why Jesus is one of the most historically verified lives of ancient times.

Dr. John Ankerberg: Welcome. If you read the articles about Jesus in national magazines such as *Time*,

Newsweek, or *U.S. News & World Report*, you know that the truth claims of Christianity are under attack. A liberal group of scholars called the Jesus Seminar have published their conclusions and stated: it is no longer credible to think of Jesus as divine, Jesus did not rise from the dead, and the New Testament is a highly biased attempt to invent Christianity. In other words, if you're a Christian and believe that Jesus is God, that he said the things recorded in the gospels, that he died on the cross and rose again from the dead, then your faith is not credible, and you have no historical evidence to back up your beliefs. Such statements are just plain wrong. My guest today is Dr. Gary Habermas, who has a Ph.D. and has written some twenty books and over 100 articles on the life of Jesus and other subjects. I asked him what mainstream scholarship thinks about the conclusions of the Jesus Seminar. Here is what he said.

Dr. Gary Habermas: Now, with respect to the Jesus Seminar, what's bothered a lot of people, and not just conservatives, is that we're talking about several dozen scholars here. But quite frequently, in interviews or elsewhere, they'll say, basically, "We're mainstream. We've got the fundamentalists over here on the right, and we've got the people who don't believe there's a Jesus at all–he never existed–on the other side, and we're in-between them, in the middle." But they're not mainstream, and they do not speak for even most scholars, as many have said.

Now regarding the historical facts, I think that if we do link ourselves to what history says, we've got a situation where we can know quite a lot of information concerning Jesus. There are dozens of facts about Jesus' birth, his life, his teachings, his death, everything–even his burial. This especially applies to his resurrection appearances. And we're not even short of information regarding claims that he was deity, both from material both inside and outside the New Testament.

Ankerberg: One of the most unfounded statements made by the Jesus Seminar is that there is no real historical evidence for the Jesus of traditional Christian beliefs. But that is simply false. Dr. Habermas lists some of the different sources where facts about Jesus can be found. Listen:

Habermas: Well, as far as the historical facts are concerned, the New Testament has always been and still remains the best source for the historicity of Jesus. This is the case even according to critical scholars who use it regularly. And maybe we can comment more on this later, but I think the case for the overall life of Jesus Christ can be built from the ground up.

I also think that we have to look beyond the New Testament at Christian claims outside the New Testament. We have to look at some dozen and a half non-Christian sources outside the New Testament. Archaeology chimes in on a few things here, as well, and when you put it all together, we have quite a lot of information about Jesus Christ and his life in the first century.

Ankerberg: Now, the Jesus Seminar claims that the New Testament documents are not historical biographies of Jesus but only theological reflections about him. But Dr. Habermas explains that other historical writings also contain theological ideas, without being disqualified as reporting historical information. Listen:

Habermas: One problem is the charge that the New Testament writers were theologians or worse and therefore just presenting propaganda. From the Greek and Roman historians of that time, we have very few historical accounts that do not include the supernatural. We really have very few ancient accounts where the authors are just plain "hardcore historians." The fact is, if you study Livy or Tacitus, or if you look at Suetonius or Pliny if you view others from roughly the time of Jesus, these Roman historians are famous for mixing omens, miracle accounts, and other supernatural stories into their histories. Tacitus has fewer of these sorts of accounts, but we can still find them in his writings. Suetonius talks rather freely about omens and the Caesars who thought that they saw their demise ahead of time, so they acted this way or that way. What do contemporary historians think about this? Sometimes they may respond with a comment like, "Well, that's different. These writers are real historians, and they're not attempting to talk theology or religion, like the Gospels writers do."

However, in principle, just because the New Testament has things to say about theology and faith, that has nothing to say about whether they can also report accurate history. There is a good amount of historical data in the New Testament, and I think that's recognized by the majority of scholars today.

Ankerberg: Next, the Jesus Seminar claims that Matthew, Mark, Luke, and John really didn't write their gospels. Further, the Jesus Seminar has concluded that only about 18 percent of the words ascribed to Jesus in the gospels were actually spoken by him. What about this? Dr. Habermas explains that (1) the traditional authors can be defended, (2) the critical scholars have conceded that parts of the gospels are historically true, and (3) you can take that evidence and easily defend traditional Christian beliefs about Jesus. Listen:

Habermas: Let me make three comments about the authorship of the gospels. First, the traditional authors, Matthew, Mark, Luke, and John, can be defended with a good deal of scholarly force, and it is still being done today. Second, British New Testament scholar R. T. France stated, for example, that even if we don't take the time to sit down and work all the way through each of the traditional authors, we can still support the authenticity of the gospels on the same ground that we do for Roman history – that these are still the earliest extended accounts about Jesus that we possess.

As such, they are due the respect of being the earliest historical pieces of data on this subject, and we should make use of them accordingly. Besides, time and again, they have been shown to present many reliable historical reports.[1]

So, we could argue for the traditional gospel authors. If scholars don't like that, the gospels still remain the earliest books that depict a large portion of Jesus Christ's public ministry and have been shown to employ reliable traditions.

But third, I prefer another type of argument that builds from the ground up, that does not take a more common approach that these books must be totally historical before they are useful, thereby making every detail in them true. Coming at this subject from a different angle than this last one, I call my method[2] the "Minimal Facts Argument" and suggest that this sort of approach is probably the strongest, in evidential terms. It employs snippets of information, basically moving one fact at a time, building a case upwards, but only when there is much factual support for each of these historical facts. It is as if

---

[1] R.T. France, *The Evidence for Jesus, The Jesus Library*, Michael Green, Series Editor (Downers Gove, IL: InterVarsity, 1986), pp. 101-111, 122-125, 133-139.

[2] Incidentally, it must be noted that this approach is precisely an apologetic method rather than any sort of personal position on the truth of the New Testament proclamation. I sometimes refer to it as the "lowest common denominator" methodology

we were building a wall, one brick at a time, with each historical fact being one of these bricks. Because of the large amount of scholarly confirmation for these particulars, critical scholars generally recognize that they are historical events.

As I explain to my graduate students over and over again, with critical scholars today, most generally, the "authentic" Pauline epistles are almost always accepted as authoritative, while the gospels frequently are questioned. On the other hand, for evangelical Christians, Paul and the gospels are all part of Scripture. But if the critical scholars are going to grant us more than a half-dozen of Paul's major epistles as being good sources, why don't we take those texts and begin building a strong case—a brick wall, as it were? So I would favor taking a number of historical facts that are recognized and accepted by virtually all scholars, building up these data and showing how we can make our case, based on these few facts alone, rather than holding out for all of the New Testament. That is the chief idea behind the Minimal Facts Argument.

Ankerberg: There is a body of Pauline literature that can be accepted as historical by virtually everyone. Let me give you an example or two. G.A. Wells is the British Professor of German who has written a number of books arguing that Jesus probably never lived. G.A. Wells will still grant eight authentic Pauline letters. But that doesn't satisfy the Christian who would like thirteen. But instead of being upset with him for what he doesn't give us, let's take what he does give us. Those eight Pauline epistles that Wells grants include our most important doctrinal works, namely, Romans, 1 and 2 Corinthians, Galatians, and Philippians. He gives you all those. And so, since in these epistles Paul is a good source, even for somebody like G.A. Wells who argues that Jesus probably never existed, then let's use Paul.

And when we're talking about the resurrection of Jesus, for an example, or the nature of the gospel, let's look at 1 Corinthians 15, let's look at Galatians 1, passages that are unanimously given. And that is precisely why the New Testament still gives us our best data because this is all a sort of irreducible minimum or the lowest common denominator. We still have plenty of data here to talk about the Jesus of history.

Some in the Jesus Seminar may think that the Apostle Paul invented the divinity of Christ; that Paul's Jesus is completely different from the historical Jesus.

What historical evidence proves is that the Apostle Paul did not invent Jesus; rather, both he and the other Apostles viewed Jesus the same way and preached the same message? Listen:

Habermas: One of the most important pieces of information that the critical community will almost unanimously admit and allow is 1 Corinthians 15. Now, in the first two verses, Paul had just said, basically, "I came to you Corinthians and I preached the gospel to you." Paul went there in person and preached orally. We're talking here about a date that is well-recognized as 51-52 AD. And Paul said, essentially, "I preached the words of the gospel. If you believe those, you're saved, and if not, you're not." [1 Cor. 15:1-2]

Then Paul defined for them the factual side of the gospel message. He states in verse 3: "For what I received, I passed on to you as of first importance: that Christ died for our sins according to the scriptures; that he was buried; that he was raised on the third day according to the scriptures, and that he appeared to Peter and then to the twelve." [1 Cor. 15:3-5] Then he listed some of the other appearances. He added at the end, "Last of all, he appeared to me." [1 Cor. 15:8] So this is one of the very clearest statements of the factual portion of the gospel message, as proclaimed in the New Testament.

Why do scholars take this text so seriously? First of all, it's from an epistle that is unanimously thought to be written by the Apostle Paul. Why is that? Well, as one scholar attested, we don't even need to discuss Pauline authorship here because both the internal and external evidence for this epistle are so strong. Like what?

Well, just prior to 100 AD, Clement of Rome wrote a letter to the Corinthians (about 95 AD). Then, just after 100 AD, Ignatius wrote seven brief epistles around 107 AD, and Polycarp wrote another one about 110 AD. These three men, writing nine short epistles, quote, cite, or refer to the book of 1 Corinthians approximately some 30 times, and do so just about a decade after the traditional close of the New Testament. That is an incredible amount of attestation from sources outside of Paul, all asserting Paul's authority. These are just some of the many reasons that cause even skeptics to admit that Paul the apostle wrote this epistle.

So, when Paul presented the report here that he received from others, namely, that "Christ died for our sins according to the scriptures, was buried, and rose again the third day and appeared . . . ." [1 Cor. 15:3-4], he must be taken seriously. And scholars do indeed take him that way, too. Further, it is admitted virtually unanimously that Paul at least believed that he saw the risen Jesus himself, and that makes all the difference in the world.

So, we're dealing with someone here who was there very close to the beginning, who knew the other Apostles, who's repeating the gospel that they all agreed on and which they all taught. In 1 Corinthians 15:11, Paul states that it therefore made no difference whether it was he or the other apostles who were presenting this gospel message, precisely because they were all preaching the same thing. Paul took great care–as he explained in Galatians 2:2 (another of Paul's unanimously-recognized epistles)–to ascertain that this was the same gospel that the other apostles were preaching, too, as the others had affirmed regarding Paul just four verses later (Gal. 2:6).

This is why eminent Cambridge University New Testament professor C.H. Dodd stated it like this: "anyone who should maintain that the primitive Christian Gospel was fundamentally different from that which we have found in Paul must bear the burden of proof." This is the case precisely because "Paul's preaching represents a special stream of Christian tradition which was derived from the mainstream at a point very near to its source."[3]

Ankerberg: Now remember, the Jesus Seminar claims Christians have *no* historical evidence for Jesus' resurrection appearances and that Paul invented the deity of Christ, but they are mistaken. These words of Paul in 1 Corinthians 15, accepted by almost all critical scholars, take us right back very close to Christ himself. Look at this timeline:

- In 30 AD, Jesus died by crucifixion.
- Shortly thereafter, Peter, James the brother of Jesus, and the other apostles preached Jesus' resurrection and deity.
- In 32 AD, Paul met the risen Christ while he was on the road to Damascus and became a Christian.
- In 35 AD, Paul went to Jerusalem to meet the apostles Peter and James and to check out his gospel to see if his message contained the same truths about Christ that the other eyewitnesses of

---

[3] C.H. Dodd, *The Apostolic Preaching and its Developments* (Grand Rapids, MI: Baker Book House, 1980, reprint), p. 16.

Jesus' life, death and resurrection also preached. The others confirmed his message.

- Then in 51 AD, Paul preached the gospel orally to people in Corinth, and many become Christians.
- In 55 AD, Paul wrote 1 Corinthians and recorded the facts that he received from the other apostles about Jesus and knew to be true himself.

This information indicates that Paul did not invent Christ's deity but that he was in agreement with the very same message that Peter and James also preached. Further, it's obvious that Peter and James were preaching their message way before Paul arrived on the scene. So, Paul couldn't have invented Jesus Christ and his message.

Dr. Habermas explains why these historical facts indicate a sound foundation about Jesus and cannot be denied. Listen:

Habermas: Let's talk about why this is so important in terms of history. 1 Corinthians 15 is nearly a given, even from people like G.A. Wells and Michael Martin, who say that Jesus probably never lived. Paul said, "I delivered unto you the gospel which I also received: Christ died for our sins, was buried, rose again on the third day and then appeared . . . ." [1 Cor. 15:1-4]

Now, let's see what this looks like on a timeline. Let's picture between my hands here a space of about 25 years: 30ish AD–the cross of Jesus; 55ish AD–the writing of 1 Corinthians. It really doesn't make a difference if you're a liberal or a conservative here, either. These dates remain the same, within a year or so. Now, Paul wrote 1 Corinthians in 55: "I delivered it to you (orally) when I came to you." [1 Cor. 15:1] When was that? About 51 AD. Now notice, we've closed the gap from 25 years to about 20 years – from 30ish to 51. Then he said, "I delivered unto you that which I also received." [1 Cor. 15:3]

Now, the ten-million-dollar question here is, when did Paul receive this material and from whom did he obtain it? There are five steps here: the cross and Paul's epistle are the outside book ends, and the oral testimony is in-between. Then we have two stages to go: when and from whom did Paul receive this creedal testimony? Of course, the folks who passed it on to him had the material before he did.

The common consensus of recent critical New Testament scholars provides the following data: Paul most likely received this material when he visited Peter and James, the brother of Jesus, in Jerusalem about 35 AD. How do they arrive at this year? Well, if the crucifixion was about 30, then scholars place Paul's experience on the road to Damascus at just about one to three years later. He said in Galatians 1:18 (again, another of Paul's authentic epistles) that he went away for three years and that, afterward, he went to Jerusalem. That's an average of two years before his conversion, plus another three years afterward, which totals five years (2 + 3 = 5 years) later for this visit.

Now, if Paul's experiences came only one year afterward, as some think, then that's one + three = four years after the crucifixion. But 35 AD is a nice round figure. So, you've got the cross at about 30, 1 Corinthians written about 55, and Paul's oral teaching in Corinth about 51. He attested that he went to Jerusalem in approximately 35, and he explained that he spent 15 days talking with Peter and James, the brother of Jesus [Gal. 1:18].

There's a helpful Greek word here, too. In English, it is usually translated as Paul "getting acquainted with Peter," or "seeing Peter" or maybe even "questioning Peter." The Greek word is *historeo*. The root word is *histor* when transliterated into English, and it's the root word for our word "history." *Histor* is used in documents outside the New Testament as when someone travels and maps out a region, for example, showing changes in the terrain and so on. A few critical word studies from non-Evangelical authors point out that this word in Galatians 1:18 basically indicates that Paul played the role of checking the testimony he received or even playing a sort of investigative reporter.

Now, if Paul went up to Jerusalem around 35 AD and met with Peter and James, the brother of Jesus, and did some checking on these apostles' Christian testimony, there's one other thing to learn. What did they talk about? One of the old rules of literary criticism is that we do best to interpret a text in its context, and the passage both before and the one immediately afterward both state that Paul was talking about the nature of the gospel message.

Does that surprise us at all? After all, when we think of it, what else would Paul rather talk about more than the gospel? He traveled all of this distance to Jerusalem in order to meet with the head apostles, including the brother of Jesus. What would your first question be if you were Paul? I think just normally, Paul would ask about the gospel. But as we said, that is also the immediate context, and Paul is basically asking, "Tell me about what happened."

Now, just a few verses later in Galatians 2:1-2, Paul stated that he went up to Jerusalem again 14 years after the first visit, or at approximately 48 AD, or some 18 years after the crucifixion. Paul went there to specifically to check out the nature of his gospel message (2:2) to see if "I was running or had run... in vain." So now Paul is attempting to ascertain whether or not he and the other apostles were on the same "gospel page," so-to-speak. As the passage relates later, the other apostles added nothing to his message (2:6) and responded by giving he and Barnabas "the right hand of fellowship." [2:9]

Lastly, we mustn't miss who gave these men this commendation: James, the brother of Jesus, Peter, and this time the apostle John was present, as well. Paul calls them the "pillars" (Gal. 2:9). Along with Paul himself, no one in the early church was more influential than these four apostles. The other three basically concluded that "Paul, you're on the right track here. We see that Jesus called you on the way to Damascus, giving you the gospel for the Gentiles. Go for it. We'll take the gospel message to the Jews." That's basically what they did in Galatians 2:6, 9. This entire sequence is crucially important.

Now, back to the original point here: 1 Corinthians– 55 AD; oral preaching in Corinth–51 AD; the crucifixion– 30 AD. With no further adjustment, that's only a total of 25ish years later, and that's quite early. But Paul got it from somebody else, and the consensus position even among critical scholars is that he most likely received it from Peter and James pretty close to 35 AD.

Now, if Peter and James gave it to Paul, then they had to have known this content before Paul did! It was their own testimony, after all, before they even met him! For years, virtually no scholars picked a date as to when these data became formalized into the early creed that we find in 1 Corinthians 15:3-7. Why not? Probably because there was no need to do so. The date basically already extended back on top of the crucifixion itself. What this shows is that the resurrection proclamation and the factual side of the gospel message as a whole (which includes at least the Deity, death, and resurrection of Jesus according to the New Testament)[4] was known, agreed upon, and shared.

In my opinion, many Evangelicals even stumble when they attest that the early apostles preached the gospel message immediately, pointing to texts like 1 Corinthians 15:1-19. True, that's only a brief 25 years later. But we can teach that Paul received this message perhaps just five years later and somebody had it before he did, going right back to the cross itself.

Now, this is one of the paths to the knowledge that the factual content of the gospel, in particular, is identified in the New Testament as at least the Deity, death, and resurrection of Jesus, as we just mentioned directly above. These are all linked to one another on exceptionally strong historical grounds. Further, critical scholars grant texts such as I Corinthians 15:1-11, and Galatians 1:18-2:10. Again, this is what I mentioned earlier—what I have called the Minimal Facts historical argument.

Ankerberg: Now, if you're a non-Christian, let me ask you, how did the Christian religion originate? How could the early Christians proclaim to the people in Jerusalem, the very city that had watched Jesus die on the cross, that Jesus was now alive? My point to you is this: there is strong historical evidence for Jesus' resurrection. It can't be ignored. Facts just don't disappear; and they are a sound foundation for a faith commitment to Jesus if you so decide. Dr. Habermas summarizes:

Habermas: Well, I hope this provides a better idea of the comment early in the program that believers indeed have a solid historical basis for our faith. We're talking about the center of Christianity, too: the Deity, death,

---

[4] For just a few of the major references, all from early passages that date even earlier than Paul, see Rom. 1:3-4, Rom. 10:9, and Philippians 2:6-11.

burial, and the resurrection of Jesus Christ. The time frame that Paul is discussing is back in the neighborhood of 35 AD, when he met with two of the central figures in the early church: Peter, the head apostle, and James, the brother of Jesus and the pastor of the Jerusalem church. This is indeed a strong foundation. So, it surprises me when I hear people saying, "Hey, there's no evidence here or there." Believers who may wonder, worry, or doubt need to be assured of these things when their faith is questioned. Let the critics deal with these sorts of data right here, found in 1 Corinthians 15 and Galatians 1-2, and the strong basis for the gospel.

Once again, we're not talking here about periphery beliefs. We're discussing the very center of our faith. Paul proclaimed that he had met the risen Jesus on the way to Damascus. Then he proceeded to check out all these things with Peter and James in Galatians 1. As if this were all not enough, he returned 14 years later in order to make *absolutely* sure that he was not preaching the wrong message and doing so in vain! But the other major, "pillar" apostles, now including John as well, assured Paul in Galatians 2 that he was on course. They attested that his message was factually grounded and true.

Then, in 1 Corinthians 15:11, Paul testified that what *they* were preaching was true: "Whether it is I or they, so we preach and so you believe." In other words, you might say that Paul was keeping watch, as well! The others had approved his message, and now he agreed with their proclamation. The wonderful conclusion is that the gospel that Paul and Barnabas preached, as well as the message taught by the other apostles, too, was one and the same. Whoever taught the message, it agreed in its core of the Deity, death, and resurrection of Jesus Christ. We're on central, sacred, and very solid grounds on these themes.

21

It would be a good exercise sometime for us to just contemplate some of these things. Is there a historical or other sort of evidential footing for any other central religious teachings of another prominent world religious founder? Prominent critical scholar John A.T. Robinson began one of his books by saying that these are not questions that are asked in the other religions, not even in the monotheistic belief systems.[5] One Buddhist scholar begins his book by declaring quite frankly that his religious tradition doesn't have anything close to Christianity's historical foundation. The texts he edited in his volume all date from 600 to 900 years after the Buddha's death! Thus, all attempts to know the Buddha's original teachings are "mere surmise" and "fruitless"![6]

---

[5] John A.T. Robinson, *Can We Trust the New Testament?* (Grand Rapids, MI: Eerdmans, 1977), p. 7.

[6] Edward Conze, Editor and Translator, Buddhist Scriptures (London: Penguin, 1959), especially pp. 11-12; cf. also p. 34.

PROGRAM 2 Is it Credible to Think of Jesus as Deity; that the Resurrection of Jesus Actually Happened?

Ankerberg: Welcome. Today liberal scholars in the Jesus Seminar are attacking traditional Christian beliefs about Jesus. They say it's no longer credible to think of Jesus as divine; the resurrection of Jesus never happened; the New Testament books do not present a historical record of Jesus but only a religious witness to early Christian beliefs. But contrary to what the Jesus Seminar says, there is a massive amount of historical information inside and outside of the New Testament that confirms traditional Christian beliefs. My guest is philosopher Dr. Gary Habermas who was himself a skeptic for years. In working on his Ph.D. at Michigan State, he came to realize that there was much solid historical evidence about Jesus that he couldn't ignore. Listen:

Habermas: In last week's program, we mentioned the very early creedal material that Paul presents in 1 Corinthians 15. This is probably the heart of contemporary discussions bearing on the historical Jesus.

Now, to summarize briefly, we said something like this: If we can imagine roughly a 25-year timeline, it would begin with the cross about 30 AD, ending with the writing of 1 Corinthians at about 55 AD. That's 25 years there. Paul reminded the church in 1 Corinthians 15:1-2 that he gave them the gospel when he came to them. That was about 51 AD, so we're at about 21 years at that point. Then in 1 Corinthians 15:3 Paul outlined some crucial creedal material, concerning which he said: "I delivered unto you that which I also received."

The typical, consensus critical view is that Paul acquired this material in Jerusalem while he met with Peter and James, the brother of Jesus, in about 35 AD (Galatians 1:18). We'd only be five years away from the cross at this point. Given that Paul received this testimony during his visit to Jerusalem, then those who "delivered" it to him had it beforehand, in order to pass it on to Paul.

One crucially important topic from last week was the question, "How do we know that Paul was not the originator of Christianity?" In the creedal tradition that Paul received as per 1 Corinthians 15:3, Paul states that this message was of "first importance," thus, it occupied the very center of his proclamation. Further, the "delivered . . . received" sequence was a formal way of passing on tradition--of declaring, among other things, that this message didn't come or originate from him.

So again, Paul passed on this gospel message as of first importance, as it occupied the center of his proclamation. Paul taught what he had received. Given that he received it in Jerusalem from Peter and James, not only is this not Paul's material, but it came from two of the important proclaimers in the early Church: Peter and James, the brother of Jesus.

How do we know that 1 Corinthians 15:3-7 is a pre-Pauline creed? Actually, there are perhaps a half dozen reasons for us to believe that this is the case. If there are any major conclusions that are unanimous in New Testament scholarship, it's probably this one. Why? For starters, remember that critical scholars think that the data indicate that Paul is a great source and that this epistle is undisputedly authentic and written by him. Further, Paul states straightforwardly that he is passing on tradition that he received personally from others, and there is no reason to disbelieve him.

One more crucial thing here concerning these words that Paul uses. It is the equivalent terms in Aramaic employed by Paul that are technical words indicating the teaching of tradition. Paul uses this structure again in 1 Corinthians 11 concerning the Lord's Supper: "delivered and received." [1 Cor. 11:23] This all makes good sense. After all, this is how Pharisees taught, and Paul was a Pharisee (Phil. 3:4-6). So, these are some pretty crucial signs that this material is not Paul's. It is pretty straightforward: if it were in existence before Paul, as about everyone thinks is the case, then it must be *pre*-Pauline!

There are several other strong indications for this conclusion being true, as well. For one thing, the text is formalized, in the sense that it appears to read in stanzas—like verses. Also, there are a number of indications that Paul is not the author of the proclamation. There are a series of non-Pauline words that Paul never uses elsewhere, such as "on the third day." Joachim Jeremias, the German New Testament scholar, argued that there's probably an Aramaic original behind the Greek text, another indication that it predates Paul.[7]

Jewish New Testament scholar Pinchas Lapide has listed at least eight indications that Paul is passing on tradition here. As another, he notes what's termed the "triple *hoti* clause." English students will recognize that as: "and that . . . and that . . . and that . . . ." Paul doesn't

---

[7] Joachim Jeremias, *The Central Message of the New Testament* (Philadelphia: Fortress Press, 1965, 1981), pp. 39-40 for some brief comments. For details, see W. Zimmerli and Jeremias, *The Servant of God* (*Studies in Biblical Study* 20), rev. ed. (London: SCM, 1965), 88ff., 95f.

come up for air until he gets this long sentence out: ". . . he died for our sins according to the scriptures *and that* he was buried *and that* he was raised *and that* he appeared." Dr. Lapide tells us that this sequence is a sign of Hebrew narration.

So, there are a number of reasons to conclude that this text is exactly as Paul states: a proclamation that he is passing on to others, though he was not its originator. Lapide additionally lists the parallelism, diction, the use of the names "Cephas" and "the twelve," and so on. These are some of the best indications that have convinced a generation of critical scholars.[8] If Paul were writing this today, he'd have been required to use a footnote!

Ankerberg: Now, some scholars in the Jesus Seminar claim that the apostle Paul is the one who invented the Jesus of faith. What they mean by this is that Paul made up the story that Jesus was God. But Dr. Habermas presents the historical facts that clearly show that Paul invented neither Christianity nor the Christ of the Christian faith. Listen:

Habermas: Now, Paul has taught several relevant things here. He stated, "I delivered what I received [and I like these next words] as of first importance." Paul basically thinks that this is the most crucial thing that he could have preached to the Corinthians. Of course, in the first two verses, he said that if they accepted this message, they were saved; if not, they weren't. So, we're right here at the center of his message. But as we have been observing clearly here, when Paul goes on to state the case that follows, the material that he presents comes straight from someone else, who gave it to him.

---

[8] Pinchas Lapide, *The Resurrection of Jesus: A Jewish Perspective*, trans. by Calwer Verlag, no name given (Minneapolis: Augsberg, 1983), pp. 97-99.

In this tradition, Jesus appeared to an individual, Peter; then to a group, called by its better-known name, the Twelve; then to 500 brethren (counting the men only?) at once. Then he appeared to James, another individual, then to another group: "all the apostles." [1 Cor. 15:5-7] There's some order to this listing, and it's arranged like a catechism.

If it were true, as it is sometimes estimated, that perhaps even as much as 90 percent of the Jews in that area were illiterate during the First Century, then how does someone pass on to them the heart of their message, as "of first importance"? The key points must be given to the folks in a form where they can memorize them and repeat them back, teaching still others, even though they may not be able to read. That is the nature of these pre-Pauline creedal passages. Paul basically proclaimed the heart of his message, the very central items he taught when he came to their city, adding further, "and folks, so you know, it's not my material."

So, in sum, I think we need to reiterate several things here: this gospel material is absolutely central, even "of first importance." It's a very early message, prior to Paul's conversion, which took place about one to three years after the crucifixion.

Since the apostolic eyewitnesses who were with Jesus had the message before Paul, we've got a timeline going back to Jesus in 30 AD. But since it's not Paul's material, he cannot be the originator of the New Testament message, and at its most important place at that.

But speaking regarding the appearances of the risen Jesus that the other apostles were also proclaiming, Paul asserts in 1 Corinthians 15:11 that, "Whether then it was I or they, this is what we preach and this is what you believed." Again, the "we" here is clearly the other apostles. Paul is asserting that, whether you hear it from them or hear it from me, we're preaching the same gospel message concerning especially the resurrection appearances in particular.

So, it seems clear that what Paul is teaching here is, "Ask the other apostles. They'll tell you the same thing I'm telling you. We're all on the same page here." But according to the previous verses, it was the other apostles who originated this message. Paul and the chief apostles already talked it over on more than one occasion, and the others commended Paul's message, according especially to Galatians 2:1-10. Remember, too; it was Paul who journeyed to Jerusalem and *sought out the others* on this topic, as well.

This is why we are at a very special junction in history where we can almost hear for ourselves what Paul is teaching, linked, as it is, through time-space history. It's his words that are on the page. He's an accredited messenger. But he is the teacher who passes out the material of others.[9]

So, we have a timeline here, and the basics are very widely recognized by non-Evangelical critical scholars. I think that by utilizing the Minimal Facts Method, then, we can observe the very firm grounds here regarding the very heart of our faith: the death, burial, and resurrection of Jesus the Christ.

Ankerberg: How many times in school have you heard that the material in the New Testament books is nothing more than legend or myth? Well, again, that's just a lie. Dr. Habermas gives three reasons why scholars

---

[9] 2 Timothy 2:2 is helpful here as another similar example from the early church, though it is a rare critic who will take this as the teaching of Paul.

believe they are dealing with solid historical evidence about Jesus. Listen:

Habermas: Now, we can slow down just a little bit here and see another angle why the 1 Corinthians 15 passage is taken so seriously by critical scholars. First, we have said at length that this material is undoubtedly very, very early. From Paul's trip to Jerusalem in 35ish AD, visiting with Peter and James, the brother of Jesus [Galatians 1:18]—to the time before that when Peter and James themselves received or even chose the wording for this creedal material, we've got hands-on material from a very early period that emphasizes the central facts regarding the very beginnings of Christianity. This is surely a window into those initial years!

It's difficult to know and appreciate how early this material is until you've worked with Greco-Roman writers from this time period. For example, the best lives of Alexander the Great that we have are dated over 400 years after he lived! 400 years! But no one talks about how we can know so very little about Alexander. And then, one of the very best Roman historians, Livy, reports things that supposedly occurred hundreds of years before his time.

In contrast, Paul is recording a list of events that he participated in just five years after the occasion. Then, others had it before Paul did, and they were even closer to the events than was Paul himself! So, we've cut down the gap here tremendously, until there's no really no gap at all! Recall, too, that this is no periphery, borderline doctrine in Christianity—it is the very gospel message itself, "of first importance" as Paul claims, and we begin to understand and appreciate this incredible picture.

Secondly, through the window of the creedal tradition and then confirmed by Paul's word, especially after what he learned from the other three chief apostles themselves (Peter, James the Lord's brother, and John), we have their eyewitness testimonies, too. Paul certainly knew how to secure eyewitness testimony—interview the participants face-to-face! Then reproduce their own verification probably in their words, as in a footnote! After all, that's the very best ancient path for formulating and teaching history, and Paul was honest enough to divulge that this was not his material. We have mentioned the authorship of the gospels, and that's another possible route to go for sources. However, pursuing Paul's method is really taking what he contributed and what is granted freely by the critical scholars.

Then don't forget another crucial truth: Paul himself was an eyewitness on this subject of the resurrected Jesus. Let's not miss the forest for the trees here. Paul told us more than once that he had seen the risen Jesus (1 Cor. 9:1; 15:8).

However, perhaps Paul's most helpful contribution of all was in passing on the testimony and confirmation of these other three apostles. Now through Paul, we've also heard from Peter as well as James, the brother of Jesus, and the apostle John. The first two, by the way, are both listed individually and immortalized as among those who saw Jesus, as reported in the creedal list here (15:5, 7). So we're dealing with the chief witnesses who were there from the very beginning.

A third way to go after this overall picture is to inquire into an entirely new area that we have not really discussed: to look at the early traditions that are found in Acts—what are known as the early sermon summaries. Ask an Evangelical, "What does the earliest Christian preaching look like prior to the writing of the first New Testament books?" They would probably say, "Simple—just read the book of Acts." If you asked some critical scholars, they might also say, "Read Acts, meaning these sermon summaries."

Now, those answers may sound very close to the same as other creeds that we have mentioned, but they are really reporting or at least emphasizing different things. Evangelicals answer this way because they trust the entire text of Acts. Critics look for and study a number of these early confessional or traditional sermonic passages in Acts. These sermon summaries—"sermonettes" if you will--are usually longer texts than the New Testament creeds that we have mentioned above and thus may be considered as a slightly different species of very early tradition. True, it is sometimes the case that they are located in the text for similar reasons.

It should be noted that most of the Acts sermon summaries are also thought to potentially have Aramaic original forms, too, similarly indicating their earlier origins. However, among the differences with the creeds in the epistles, some of the sermon summaries also tend to be longer than the briefer theological creeds in the epistles. In that sense, their length makes them appear a little more similar to the early hymns of Philippians 2 and Colossians 1. Also, there is a little more difference between commentators over which verses within each of these chapters are the exact kernel of the early messages.

One example of a sermon summary is thought to be the presence of shorter, more compact, seemingly unevolved theology. The thought is that undeveloped theology is an indication of earlier layers of preaching. For example, one such scene in Acts that is often thought to be such a sermon summary is when Peter says (and you can almost picture him pointing at the Jewish leaders as he speaks): "You killed him! God raised him from the dead!" [Acts 3:15] Here's another pithy saying: "We ought to obey God rather than man." [Acts 5:29] The key candidates for these sermon summaries are found in Acts 1-5, and Acts 10, which are Petrine. Acts 13 and Acts 17 appear to include other texts of a Pauline nature, though scholars do not seem to cite them quite as frequently as the Petrine examples.[10] Still, any such conclusions that these are early sermon summaries are obviously very helpful as additional sources, as well.

Among the most crucial portions of this discussion is that, in every encapsulation of the gospel message that is found in these texts, the Deity of Christ (a time or two this theme is more implied), along with his death, and his resurrection are found quite explicitly. Many critical scholars doubt that Paul is the actual author of the actual summaries in Acts 13 and 17. So once again, if these summaries date to the 30s, those would also be independent and pre-Pauline sources. Still, Dodd, a recognized authority on these matters, points out that the summaries, in general, are so close to Paul's teachings in his epistles that this is still another indication of how early and apostolic Paul's teaching is to the original source. His is definitely not a separate strand of thought.[11]

So for a number of reasons, then, Paul's teachings definitely did not constitute the origin of early Christianity. Most of these best-known candidates for early Christian preaching snippets predate Paul, whose teachings do not even emerge on the scene until the first account of his trip to Damascus in Acts 9. Five chapters (Acts 1-5) before that contain this early preaching material, including the same fundamental message, although Paul is not around.

---

[10] We will list below many of these specific passages in Acts.

[11] Dodd, The Apostolic Preaching and its Developments, especially 26, 31.

Dodd summarizes the chief themes of the four major Petrine sermon summaries in Acts 2-5, and finds most prominently the ideas of preaching the Messianic fulfillment in the dawning Kingdom of God, the ministry, Deity, death, and resurrection of Jesus, and the resurrection as the chief indicator that Jesus is the exalted Lord. We could still go to these chapters in Acts and find in them something quite close to: "This is the message of first importance, how that Jesus died, was raised and appeared, and more than being the man Jesus, he is also Lord and Christ." All of this is from Peter and company prior to Paul's appearing on the scene.[12]

So, going at it from this third angle of Acts, we have these sermon summaries with these unevolved, short, concise, succinct theological statements of the gospel message, and Paul is not even around yet. So, here's another way to look at the center of the Christian core, the gospel of salvation, earlier than and apart from Paul. But let's be clear: when Paul comes on the scene, as Dodd said, his message follows the previous apostolic pattern, which is major.

Now, back to Dr. Ankerberg's question: did Paul make this all up himself? Was he the father of the most important Christian doctrines? Hardly. The answer, of course, is definitely not, because all of these crucial points that were "of first importance" came from someone else, as he explained and acknowledged freely in his own teachings.

Ankerberg: Now, every Christian student should listen carefully to how Dr. Habermas is arguing. As Christians, we all accept the New Testament books as authoritative and true. But your non-Christian professor

---

[12] Dodd, Ibid., especially pp. 20-24.

and friends don't. Well, then, what evidence should you use in talking to them? If your professor and friends are up on modern scholarship, they know that certain portions of Paul's writings and portions of the four gospels are accepted, not as inspired, but as historically reliable information. Now, if they accept it, then let's use that material because it reveals the historical facts that Jesus lived, claimed to be God, died on a cross, was buried in a tomb, and appeared to his disciples later. This is historical evidence which can't be ignored. Now, if you ask, what are some of those passages that virtually all critical scholars accept that tell us these things? Dr. Habermas explains. Listen:

Habermas: So, we've kind of come through the back door. We've started with the data that are definitely the strongest: like 1 Corinthians 15 and Paul's undisputed epistles. We've moved backwards about 25 years from the date of 1 Corinthians to the crucifixion. We've taken a look at Peter and James the brother of Jesus through Paul's eyes, in Galatians 1:18-20. Then in Galatians 2:1-10 these same three apostles plus John were present several years later and they confirmed the nature of the gospel message that they were all preaching and teaching. The other apostles did not adjust any of Paul's actual gospel message (Gal. 2:2-9). We also took a little bit of a detailed look at some of the major themes of the Petrine sermon summaries or snippets in the early chapters of Acts.

The more radical community of scholars way over on the left does not generally like the gospels, except for some brief texts here and there when they are confirmed by various checks and balances. Yet they defend and accept the so-called "authentic" seven or so Pauline epistles. These radical scholars sometimes claim that they hold mainstream views, but almost no one accepts that such is the case. However, there's also a moderate community of scholars out there in-between the scholars of the left and right, to which probably the most influential scholars belong right now. In general, they would recognize the historicity of many individual gospel accounts, including some of major importance.

Let me make this point again. 1 Corinthians predates the gospels, and 1 Corinthians 15 is the longest extended treatment of the resurrection before the four gospels. So really, on the timeline, the gospels were written later. So here we've got the chronological horse of Paul's epistles in the right place, before the gospel cart. If it's already in Paul, and if the earliest Acts sermon summaries are also confirmation, why are many critical scholars objecting to the gospels when we've already got it in the earlier timeline in Paul's "authentic" epistles and the Acts sermon summaries?

When you check out the gospels, do you hear these same major themes? When Jesus speaks, and the events unfold, do you hear the same basic, overall proclamation on key themes like who Jesus claims to be, the nature and duration of God's kingdom, the crucifixion, and the resurrection appearances? This is why we cited Dodd's comment earlier that the apostolic streams did not veer very far away from each other.[13]

When Paul visited Jerusalem, his world, and that of the other apostles came together. Paul got to hear from people who knew Jesus intimately. He talked to the lead apostle, Peter. He talked to James, Jesus' own brother. In the next visit in Galatians 2, when Paul returned to Jerusalem, he found these same two apostles there again (Peter and James), plus John the Apostle was also present. So, Paul's got some connections!

---

[13] Dodd, Ibid., p. 16; cf. 21, 26, 31.

On another absolutely vital subject, Paul did not invent the deity of Christ, either, as we sometimes hear. Lofty titles for Jesus do in fact appear all over Paul's "authentic" epistles. But they are also found in the early sermon summaries in Acts, and perhaps most importantly, in the pre-Pauline creedal statements that are earlier than Paul's epistles themselves, such as those found in Romans 1:3-4, 10:9, 1 Corinthians 8:6, or Philippians 2:6-11.

But we find these titles in the gospels, too, in the teachings of Jesus himself. Many scholars think that our two best grounds for talking about the deity of Christ in the gospels are Jesus' self-designations "Son of Man" and "Son of God." Now, Son of God is more easily and usually recognized to be a title of deity. But Son of Man shouldn't be said to refer only to Jesus' human nature, or something like that. To summarize some scholarship real briefly here, Jesus shows that he knows the passage in Daniel 7:13-14 where Daniel sees a vision of the Ancient of Days, and one coming down from him, who looks like a Son of Man.

The idea had emerged in some Jewish writings of about this time, non-Christian texts that had nothing to do with Scripture. The Son of Man could be a human being as in the Psalms, or it might designate a prophet as in the book of Ezekiel, or it can be the Son of Man who comes down from the Ancient of Days. Daniel's usage is of a prophetic figure whom critical scholars often identify as preexistent and divine, who sets up God's Kingdom on earth.

Which of these three senses does Jesus employ for himself? Son of Man is Jesus' favorite self-designation in the gospels and at least twice, one of them in Mark 14, he basically paraphrases some of the vital elements of Daniel 7:13-14. Then he clearly identifies himself as that last person. The Jewish high priest asks Jesus, "Are you the Christ [Messiah], the Son of the Blessed One?" Notice

Jesus' response: *Ego eimi*, "I am." Then Jesus changes a Son of God question to a Son of Man answer. He basically retorts, "I am the Christ, the Son of God, and you will see the Son of Man sitting on God's right hand and coming with the clouds of heaven [in judgment]." [Mark 14:60-62]

Here the priest made a formal declaration of blasphemy. He ripped his garment and declared that Jesus had committed blasphemy. The other leaders present agreed with him that Jesus was definitely worthy of death. They thought they had him at last [v. 63]!

Now, what set off the high priest? Of our three Old Testament notions of the son of man, this is by far the closest to Daniel 7:13-14. In this passage in Mark 14, Jesus responded, *Ego eimi*, as in "I am the Son of God." Then he said that, as the Son of Man, he would be seen sitting on God's right hand and coming with the clouds of heaven. So, Jesus claimed to be the preexistent one who came from the Ancient of Days to set up God's Kingdom. He also used the enigmatic phrase, "coming with the clouds." That phrase is used often in the Old Testament as a reference to God. But scholars often agree that claiming to sit on God's right hand was the most serious and blasphemous claim of the entire passage.

The high priest responded almost as if he had been waiting all along, or perhaps dearly hoping, for something just like this clear affirmation. In contemporary terms, instead of tearing his clothing, he might have responded with an energetic fist-pump in the air, followed by something like, "Yeah, we've got him now. He's going to die for this." He could also very well have thought that this was a case of mano e mano, and although all of his other witnesses had failed to do the job properly, he was the high priest, and he had made the charge stick! Little did he know at the time that he probably gave us the clearest expression of all of our texts that Jesus had plainly claimed to be Deity!

So, if Jesus himself claimed to be both the Son of God as well as the Son of Man, why do some say that Paul invented the Deity of Christ? We see Jesus' own teachings in the gospels. We find them in the pre-Pauline creeds that even pre-date Paul's earliest epistles, as well as in the early brief sermon summaries in Acts. Of course, they are found in Paul's uncontested epistles, too. I think this is a solid case for the deity of Christ from the earliest of times. There are other arguments here, as well, but these will have to suffice for right now.

But if Christ was raised from the dead, now we've got to ask the question, "What is God showing us here?" The traditional Christian response, starting with the New Testament itself, is that God's raising Jesus indicates that Jesus' Father confirmed his Son's message. Remember, Dodd finds it in the earliest Acts sermon summaries. Now, if Jesus had claimed to be deity but was not, nothing could be more blasphemous than usurping God's nature and personal place in the universe.

But since he clearly did claim it and was subsequently raised from the dead, this event serves as God's stamp of approval on Jesus' teachings. This argument shows up on the lips of Peter according to the preaching texts in Acts 2:22-28 and 4:2, as well as by Paul in Acts 17:29-31, and in the pre-Pauline creedal statement in Romans 1:3-4. The resurrection is the capstone. As Paul declared in 1 Corinthians 15:3a, it truly is a matter of first importance, and as he affirms later, the resurrection drives home the truth of the theology.

Ankerberg: Now, if the Jesus Seminar scholars were listening to what Dr. Habermas was saying, how would they respond? He tells us. Listen:

Habermas: In this program, we've been talking a little bit concerning the Pauline and pre-Pauline aspects of a historical timeline that extends from approximately 55 back to 30 AD. We've concentrated particularly on the first five-year block, or from about 35 back to 30 AD.

I mentioned that Paul focused on the truth and the nature of the gospel proclamation while he was speaking with Peter and James, the brother of Jesus, and again in his later visit with these same two apostles, plus the apostle John, as well. We also discussed some of the sermon summaries in Acts, where the gospel data are almost always central to the discussion. We ended by addressing one of the more highly evidenced texts in the gospels, emphasizing what Jesus said regarding himself.

These ideas were quite similar to the earlier teachings, as well. Sure, I'll guess what some of the more extreme critical scholars are going to shake their heads and say in response: "Habermas has slaughtered gospel studies here.

He thinks that just because the gospels report that Jesus said something, that he truly must have said just that. But what could be more of a myth than a man's claim to be Deity? Simply take a look at the Greek heroes. Or just read some of the Roman authors."

You know, this is a worthwhile challenge to address, too. It could easily fill a program by itself. How do we know, in fact, that Jesus really did claim to be the Son of God and the Son of Man? Now, we're getting close to the center, and if we've got Jesus himself teaching these truths, not to mention the pre-Pauline creeds and the Acts sermon summaries, then certainly Paul is not the author of invented tales regarding Jesus Christ being Deity. He was still persecuting the church in these earliest days of the church!

PROGRAM 3 Did Jesus Ever Consider Himself to be Deity? Did Jesus Designate Himself as the Son of Man or the Son of God?

Ankerberg: Welcome. Do you think Jesus ever considered himself to be God? The handful of liberal scholars in the Jesus Seminar claim that Jesus never said he was God. Further, they claim that later Christians deliberately excluded other books, other gospels, which pictured Jesus differently than the books which are now part of the New Testament canon. As you'll hear in this program, the Jesus Seminar is wrong on both points.

Well, let's begin with the statement, "Jesus claimed to be God." Can Christians use the Jesus Seminar's own critical methodology to examine the evidence and still prove that Jesus *did* claim to be God? The answer is, "Yes." Dr. Gary Habermas, a philosopher, and historian, has written over 100 articles of various sorts for scholarly journals, many of these on the Historical Jesus. As a Christian, there are many reasons that have led him to accept all of the content in the New Testament books as true and authoritative. But he knows non-Christian scholars do not believe the same way. So he starts with the snippets of material in the New Testament that they do accept as authoritative and historically reliable and uses that material to prove that Jesus did refer to himself as God.

Now, Dr. Habermas argues that no matter which source, which stratum New Testament critics turn to in the Gospels, in all five of them you'll find that Jesus designates himself as Son of Man, which, as you'll see, is a very lofty reference according to Daniel 7:13-14. So listen as Dr. Habermas uses the critics' own arguments to show Jesus did claim to be Deity.

Habermas: We ended the last program by mentioning the critical comeback that seemed obvious enough that we need to provide an answer. That objection went something like this: "Don't take it for granted that the red-letter editions of the New Testament are exactly what Jesus said. How do you know that Jesus actually proclaimed what Mark recorded, or that Matthew, Luke, or John got it right when each of them cited Jesus' teachings?"

Let me try a popular analogy for comparison. When fans and critics alike take a sort of Monday morning quarterback approach to the important football games of the previous day, it might sound something like this. They may gather on Monday morning for coffee or in the barbershop and recast yesterday's football game in their own image. "You know, if the coach had simply done this instead of that, we would have won the game." "Sure the quarterback gained some yards when he sprinted down the field, but if he would have just stayed in the pocket like he should have done, he wouldn't have gotten injured. He gained the yards but lost the trophy. Now we're out of the playoffs for sure."

In a way, this seems close to what a lot of critics say. At least since Bultmann, the gospel writers are regularly said to be placing many words and teachings into Jesus' mouth, but after his crucifixion rather than before. They are utilizing their post-Easter, Monday morning renditions of how these teachings came about. They are Monday-morning quarterbacking Jesus' teachings. But just like Monday's football plays never happened on the field, neither did those words come out of Jesus' mouth prior to the crucifixion. Similarly, how do we know the Son of Man is not just an added teaching?

Now, I provided a couple of arguments during the last program that Jesus claimed to be both the Son of Man and the Son of God. Let's take a look at a couple of these points, doing so according to critical methodology. What if we employed a method utilizing the lowest common denominator, like that which the more critical scholars do? To them, the New Testament texts are simply books of ancient literature. Okay, so critics often assume that the gospels, some of the epistles, and other New Testament writings are simply unreliable. Let's think about this like the critics do, and let's initially address the issue, "Did Jesus ever claim to be the Son of Man?" What critical indications do we have?

Two important criteria of authenticity, as they are termed by the critical scholars themselves, are both fulfilled by the Son of Man sayings in the gospels. The first one is multiple attestation: if you have a teaching of Jesus that is found in more than one independent source, you have a pretty good idea that this may be an authentic statement. In fact, the Jesus Seminar themselves list that criterion in the beginning of their book entitled *The Five Gospels*, that rejects over 80% of the so-called red-letter sayings of Jesus. They state that just *two* independent sources increase the odds of authenticity.

What about the teaching that Jesus was the Son of Man? Not only is it Jesus' favorite self-designation, according to the gospels, but it is found in all five of what are often termed the traditional gospel sources or strata! These traditional gospel sources, by the way, are the Gospel of Mark; "M"–the special material that Matthew includes that none of the others include; "L"–the special material that Luke has alone; the Gospel of John; and this enigmatic "sayings document" that critical scholars call

"Q," which is their name for the verses that are contained in both Matthew and Luke, but which are not found in Mark. So, we have five independent sources of material and guess what? The Son of Man teaching appears in all five strata! So, five out of five sources are what some scholars might call overkill—it would seem to be quite clear that Jesus actually utilized this title for himself.

But could the Christian church have made it up, and Monday morning quarterbacked it into Jesus' mouth like Monday's football play that never happened? Perhaps the Son of Man was simply the most popular title for Jesus when the gospels were written, decades later, so that they could add it back into Jesus' mouth after the fact? We'll check that out.

But then there is the second criterion, called "the criterion of dissimilarity." Some think that it is the most stringent test of all. If a teaching of Jesus was not taken from the Jews, and if the same teaching was not found in the early Church, it is probably uniquely authentic to Jesus himself. This is really quite a severe test, for it borders on asserting that we cannot be sure that a saying was actually the teaching of Jesus if either the Jews (which he, of course, was one!) or the early Christians (his own followers!) taught the same thing!

Well, didn't the Jews have a concept of the Son of Man at about Jesus' time? Sure, they did, but the non-Christian Jews of the first century would never have applied the title to Jesus.

Then what about the early Church? Isn't this supposed to be a great example of Monday morning quarterbacking? Christians read their favorite designation back into the mouth of Jesus, so that means that it was the favorite designation for Jesus when the gospels are written decades after the crucifixion. But it clearly does not work!

43

It doesn't work because Jesus is never once called the Son of Man in any of the New Testament epistles! In fact, he's not called the Son of Man anywhere outside the gospels except one place (Acts 7), and there it's talking about Stephen looking up before he was martyred and seeing the heavenly, exalted Son of Man! In fact, the text says that Stephen saw him standing on the right hand of God.

So, the earthly Son of Man, the earthly Jesus, is never called the Son of Man anywhere else outside the gospels and only on the lips of Jesus inside the gospels, except in one instance in John 12:34 where the crowd simply uses Jesus' own phrase and asked him who was the son of man? So it's a title distinctly on the lips of Jesus alone. In other words–let me unpack this just a little bit more–it couldn't be a Monday morning teaching read back into the words of the human Jesus because then it would be the church's favorite title for him at that time, but it's not found in the early church except in Stephen's vision!

So, the conclusion here, first of all, is that the title is very impressively found in all five layers of the gospel sources or strata; therefore, it far more likely goes back to Jesus himself. Second, it can't be a name given to Jesus by the Jews, and neither can it be attributed to the church, as their favorite early title for him. You know what? It looks as if Jesus must really have called himself the Son of Man!

Also, I'll just note here briefly in passing that in Mark 2:1-12, Jesus claimed that, as the Son of Man, he had the power and authority to forgive sins! This was quickly declared to be blasphemy by the Jewish elders who were present, so they understood the point. This passage is respected by critical scholars because it is one of the so-called Q texts in Matthew and Luke, which they rate quite highly.[14]

But now we've got another problem because the Son of Man of Daniel 7:13-14 is a very special figure, as we've said before. He was sent by the Ancient of Days. Critical scholars point out that this person is a preexistent, divine figure setting up God's Kingdom on Earth. If Jesus claimed to be that figure, as in Mark 14:61-64, and someone doesn't want to believe in the Deity of Christ, that at least seems like a serious enough reason for them to reconsider their position. Still, many or perhaps even most critical scholars still reject it!

Ankerberg: Now, did Jesus ever just come out and assert that he was the Son of God? What is the evidence for this? Again, Dr. Habermas takes the critics' own assumptions, points out evidence about Jesus from the critical sources or layers of historical information itself, and shows that they reveal that Jesus said he was the Son of God, too. Listen:

Habermas: Now, this second title, and as I mentioned in the earlier program, seems more obviously to be a title of deity, if Jesus called himself that. Did Jesus ever refer to himself as the Son of God?

Let me reflect on a few passages here that are very helpful in making the case that Jesus referred to himself in this manner. Again, we have to be able to rule out Monday-morning quarterbacking from the writings of the early Christian community, as well.

---

[14] Even highly critical New Testament scholar Norman Perrin of the University of Chicago counts this passage as most likely being historical, due to the criterion of multiple attestation. (Rediscovering the Teaching of Jesus [New York, N.Y.: Harper and Row, 1967], p. 29).

First, let's begin with Matthew 11:27 and its parallel saying in Luke. Here we have a passage that comes once again from the so-called "Q" passages that are found in Matthew and Luke but are absent from Mark. Critical scholars often treat these texts, along with the gospel of Mark, as the earliest gospel testimonies of all. Of course, they think that the "Q" sayings predate Matthew and Luke in order to be quoted in them. But some scholars hold that this source predates these two gospels by decades. Yet in Matthew 11:27 and its parallel, Jesus states clearly that the Father is the only one to know the son and the son is the only one who knows the Father: "No one knows the Son except the Father, and no one knows the Father except the Son and those to whom he will reveal him."

In this teaching, Jesus is claiming to possess unique knowledge of his Father, who is God, and that he is in effect the "Son of the Father." Since this is found in the very early "Q" strata, according to the way the critics view this, it's a very tough text to just simply ignore. It is sometimes even called the "Johannine thunderbolt" because it sounds like the high, exalted Christology found in the Gospel of John, in spite of being of much earlier origin!

Next, another prominent text is Mark 14:36, and here Jesus calls his Father "Abba." A lot has been written about this term, including by the prominent German New Testament scholar of a few decades ago, Joachim Jeremias, who claimed that Abba is a very special term. In his very influential argument, he made the case that there was not a single example of this usage found in the Palestinian Jewish community. Jeremias translates Abba as "dear Father" and calls it "new and unheard of" as "the claim of a unique revelation and a unique authority." But it's in

Aramaic, Jesus' language, and thereby seems to be Jesus' exact words.[15]

Let's make a really quick reference here to Mark 12:1-12, too. Jesus tells a parable where a nobleman's son was killed by wicked tenants. Mark explains that the Jewish leaders who were present knew that Jesus spoke the parable against them. Incidentally, as a parable, this passage would also count as another criterion--multiple forms—for a Son of God teaching.

So far, we have a statement from the so-called early "Q" verses in Matthew and Luke, an Aramaic reference to "Abba," and now one of the strongest statements of all: Mark 13:32. Now, one might be stunned at a first read, thinking, "What's Jesus' point here? How can this be a verse about his claiming to be Deity? In the very same context where Jesus indicates again that he is the Son of the Father, he states that he doesn't even know the time of his coming? So, no one knows the time of his return, not even Jesus himself, but only God?"

But the apparent difficulty here and the seeming reason for the consternation is exactly what makes it such a strong text that Jesus called himself the Son of the Father in this context. Here's the key point: how could we even imagine that the church invented this saying by placing these words back onto the lips of Jesus after the fact, when, by so doing, they are clearly, simply, and straightforwardly asserting something that seems to go against the very fiber of the teaching itself? Why wouldn't they just make Jesus say that he is the Son of God and leave it at that? But why say something in the immediate context that seems so seemingly contradictory, raising the question: "You mean

---

[15] Jeremias, The Central Message of the New Testament, see Chap. 1, "Abba," particularly pp. 16, 30 for his conclusions.

you're the Son of God but you don't know something, even concerning yourself?"

It is very widely agreed that this situation simply appears to be theologically embarrassing. What early Christians would make that up about Jesus? If they wanted to invent a saying that Jesus called himself the Son of God, then just come right out and say it: "And Jesus answered and said, `Behold, I'm the Son of God.'" But no!

They've got to go and announce in the exact same text, just a few words away, "and I don't know the time of my coming." Who would invent a saying like that on Monday morning and place it in the mouth of their Lord and Master?

Many find this saying to be very difficult. But the fact of the difficulty itself indicates that the best conclusion is that Jesus actually said this—these are his teachings. He indeed stated that he was the Son of the Father. Any other conclusion of a fabricated saying is simply more embarrassing for the "Monday morning church crowd." The issue of why Jesus didn't know the time of his coming may raise immediate flags for some, but it is not difficult to explain at all. I cannot pause here on this, but this is not the only time in the New Testament that states that Jesus grew in his knowledge (examples include Lk. 2:52; Heb. 5:8-9), indicating that he did not know something prior to his learning it.

But be that as it may, that statement in Mark 13:32 certainly appears to be too embarrassing to have been made by anyone other than Jesus himself. In other words, it is such a difficult sentence that, by critical standards, Jesus must have been the one who said it.

So then, we have a "Q" statement, a comment calling the Father "Abba," and we have Jesus saying that he is the Son of the Father in a very embarrassing context. I think in each of those cases that we have strong evidence that Jesus did claim to be the Son of God, just as the gospels proclaim.

Ankerberg: Now, once again, we want to drive home the point that using the critical scholars' own assumptions, you can show that Jesus claimed to be God. That doesn't mean we agree with their assumptions; it just means that the historical evidence is so strong, non-Christians can come to believe in Christ by examining these facts. Dr. Habermas summarizes this point. Listen:

Habermas: Perhaps we should backtrack here just a little bit and talk about theological definitions and, in particular, the method that I'm employing here. My point is this. If you take the traditional view of Jesus Christ as laid out in the gospels at face value, in the red letter editions, obviously no one is going to dispute the fact that Jesus in those texts claims to be the Son of God, died on the cross for our sins, and was raised from the dead.

However, I'm taking a different approach, what I might call the "Minimal Facts Method." It is what I sometimes call that "lowest common denominator" approach. I'm saying that, even if the critics were correct about their own methodology and can note, say, five layers of tradition behind the four gospels, we can make very good use of these texts alone. After all, we are utilizing actual gospel texts, such as Matthew 11:27, Mark 14:36, and Mark 13:32. In each of these passages, Jesus is making a claim to be Deity. We've also talked about exceptionally early New Testament creedal traditions along with some early Acts sermon summaries that also clearly make lofty claims about Jesus.[16]

---

[16] It should be noted that when arguing for the New Testament texts where Jesus or others are discussing his Deity, the amount of critical

Evangelicals sometimes question such a piecemeal approach, asking, "Hey, look--this whole book is Scripture. Why do we have to look at pieces?" But the critic who views the New Testament as just a book of ancient literature and perhaps nothing more is looking for the earliest, best-attested statements in support of whatever topic we are studying. And since we are doing apologetics here, we wish to put our strongest foot forward.

Remember also that many Scripture passages specifically tell us that some earlier statements are being used that predate the books in which they appear. Paul clearly states that he passed along the material that he had received from others, a report that he took to be a central matter of first importance. (I Cor. 15:3) He states almost the same words concerning another tradition in 1 Corinthians 11:23. Many other times, too, we also read comments regarding the existence and passing on of prior traditions.[17]

Lastly, when evangelicals preach or teach, they may even speak regularly from a series of key texts extracted from anywhere in Scripture, too. Really, what's the difference in commenting on or even isolating these specific passages?

The bottom line in this discussion is that we have a number of texts in the synoptic gospels that, according to critical methodology, support Jesus having called himself both the Son of Man and the Son of the Father. Add to this that we also discussed in some detail perhaps the major text (Mk. 14:61-64) where Jesus affirmed being both the

---

scholars who agree with the claims is not as unanimous as with the texts pertaining to the end of Jesus' life.

[17] Besides the texts in 1 Corinthians 11:23ff. and 15:3ff., some other examples include 1 Timothy 1:15, 3:1, 4:9, 2 Timothy 2:11, and Titus 3:8.

Son of the Blessed One as well as the Son of Man in the previous program, including sitting on God's right hand. These references are supported by brief creedal confessions that are early, predating the books in which they are written, and also confirm these designations. All of these early creedal comments could well be apostolic in nature and seem to be precisely that at least in the case of 1 Corinthians 15:3ff.

So even if all we had were the critically ascertained, lowest common denominator methods, we still have excellent reasons to think that Jesus called himself the Son of God. Even the use of critical methods fails to displace this last argument. We really can arrive at some of the strongest arguments for the Deity, death, burial, and resurrection of Jesus in this manner.

Ankerberg: Now, one of the most outrageous claims being made by members of the Jesus Seminar and other critics today is that the 27 books that now make up the canon of the New Testament were chosen for political reasons, not because these books were known and accepted for good reasons by the early Christians. It is often claimed that Christians purposely suppressed other books and gospels about Jesus that depicted Jesus in a far different way than did Matthew, Mark, Luke, and John. One of the books that some claim was purposely kept out of the canon was the *Gospel of Thomas.* But Dr. Habermas shows such claims are not true, that the *Gospel of Thomas* wasn't even in existence before 150 AD, and all the books in the New Testament were written before 100 AD. So the book of *Gospel of Thomas* couldn't be part of the canon. Listen:

Habermas: You know, John, this is one of responses that really sets me off. So we have, at the very least, the critically-ascertained portions of the gospels that we have been addressing here, plus the sermon summaries in Acts, plus the pre-Pauline creeds in various epistles, plus what critical scholars call Paul's "authentic" or "undisputed" epistles. Critics accept these six or seven Pauline epistles as authoritative texts—not as in any way inspired, but as generally reliable. These epistles are among the key portions, in apologetic terms, of the traditional canon. It looks like we are on solid ground at these points here. And the moderate critical scholars will largely agree with these sources, as well.

But what about those scholars, whoever they are, whether in the Jesus Seminar or elsewhere, who want to tell us that we kept other books out of the canon by political moves such the big guys vetoing the little guys by might since the other books didn't see eye-to-eye with them? So in spite of the other unorthodox sources being in existence, orthodox gatekeepers wanted their notion of Jesus to "win," so they orchestrated and pulled strings behind the scenes in order to mold the canon to their own liking. The *Gospel of Thomas* may be the best example of what is sometimes said to have been purposely disallowed. So, why were some books "disallowed"? Let's make *Thomas* our test case here–why was it kept out of the canon?

A few things need to be addressed right upfront. First, no matter what is decided with regard to other writings, we must *still* deal with the evidence that we have already discussed from a) the pre-Pauline creeds, b) the Acts sermon summaries, c) Paul's authentic epistles, and d) select, well-evidenced gospel passages like those we have singled out above. Whether or not there are other texts, these have to be accounted for, first and foremost. After all, Peter, John, James the brother of Jesus, and Paul are all apostles and eyewitnesses (though Paul may well only have been with regard to his own resurrection experience). So this is an especially crucial foursome with regard to the central gospel message, as laid out in Galatians 1:18-2:10. The four apostolic testimonies coincided with one another nicely.

Second, no one thinks that the *Gospel of Thomas* was written by the Apostle Thomas or anyone even close to him. So, the traditional canon at this juncture is clearly superior and more authoritative. What does "more authoritative" mean in this context? The core of texts that we enumerated directly above are written by the witnesses who were clearly in the closest proximity to Jesus.

Third, how about this idea that there was some sort of political move to keep out other books like *Thomas*? In 100 AD, a few years after the latest canonical book was completed, there couldn't have been such a political move involved, *simply because there were no books at that time like* Thomas *that could be kicked out of the canon*! The power brokers couldn't have decided, "Mark is in, but the *Gospel of Thomas* is out. Why? Because the *Gospel of Thomas* didn't even exist at that time—it wasn't even written yet!

If members of the Jesus Seminar or anyone else care to date *Thomas* earlier, especially the occasional comment that it might be a few decades earlier, it is distinctly a minority position. Of course, minority positions could turn out to be correct. But we're not basing this on guesswork here. Where are their data for this? I want the same level of evidence for *Thomas* that we had to produce for the orthodox sources listed above. "Could be" and "Maybe so" simply don't cut it!

It appears to many scholars that something else entirely is going on here. More critical scholars strongly desire rival views of Jesus. They are tired of the orthodox majority and want alternatives badly, just as in other areas of our society as a whole. But many scholarly publications have shown that these alternatives are simply nowhere to be found at this early date. So, these radical scholars tend to push and push, where innuendo and the slightest hint are often boldly juxtaposed alongside very early and credible orthodox sources

For example, "early" is a term that is sometimes used very loosely in these contexts, even indicating texts that were written in the Second or even the Third Centuries AD, rather than just 30-35 AD or just a very few years after that, as we have been using them. These critical scholars have nothing like these earlier and authoritative texts.

By far, the majority of scholars date *Thomas* in the second century. So once again, the reason nobody made a decision against *Thomas* in 50, 60, 80, or 100 AD is because there was no *Thomas*, according to almost everyone.

So, there's no choice of an orthodox canon of books dated before 100 AD where people could decide, "This is it. We're only going to take these writings, and we'll throw out the ones over there that we don't like." I'd like to know: what books were in the other pile that was cast away? And when are they being dated?

Let's view the argument the other way around, by switching sides. Evangelicals would be absolutely laughed out of court if we argued something like these critics do: "We've got a few books here that we need to have considered along with the rest. True, they may well date about a half-century to a century or more later than the latest of the earlier ones, but we need to be more inclusive here. Why can't this be a "big tent" of views, and then everyone can simply pick the Jesus they want to follow? It's just so prejudicial not to include our later texts in the canon."

Do you know what critics would probably say if *their* sources were the earliest? "Don't you think that one hundred years late is just a *little bit too* late to be an early source for the life of Jesus? I suppose you'd propose alternate, unhistorical views of George Washington, as well!" That's the chief problem for *Thomas*. The reason it's rejected in the canon is because it's too late to be very helpful. It's not rejected because someone didn't like the politics or because they didn't like any unorthodox views in the canon. First and foremost, it is simply too late. It cannot be shown that we had several pictures of Jesus making the rounds between 50 and 100 AD. It cannot be shown that the authoritative Jesus is other than that represented by his apostles such as Peter, John, James, and Paul. The *Gospel of Thomas* simply wasn't written between those years.

Ankerberg: Now, how would you show a non-Christian that the 27 books making up the New Testament are truthful books about Jesus, that they were accepted by eyewitnesses of Jesus' life, such as the apostles, and known to be authoritative books by Christians who knew the apostles? Well, there is solid, historical evidence that forms the foundation for our trust in these books. Listen:

Habermas: I'd like to say one other thing about the early canon. We have been dealing primarily with two sets of books here: the four gospels plus Acts (with Acts traditionally being viewed as volume 2 of Luke), and Paul's epistles. That's five books in the first block. Critical scholars will grant as authoritative about seven of Paul's epistles, while conservatives want to count all thirteen epistles as Paul's. But there are signs that these two sets or blocks of books were already viewed as being authoritative at the end of the first century AD. Nobody waited until Nicaea in 325 AD to begin producing a list of canonical books.

Take these three early Christian writers that we mentioned earlier: Clement of Rome's epistle to the Corinthians, written about 95 AD, Ignatius' seven epistles written about 107 AD on the way to his martyrdom, and Polycarp's Philippians, written about 110 AD. There are nine brief epistles here. These authors cite, quote, or otherwise refer to Paul and his epistles just short of a hundred times. Further, they cite 12 of the 13 epistles that bear Paul's name. The only one they leave out is Philemon, which is only one chapter long and largely non-theological. But in these references, Paul is called an apostle and inspired. His epistles are quoted right there at just before and just after approximately 100 AD by three authoritative writers.

These same ancient authors quote, cite, or otherwise refer to sayings that are found in the gospels and Acts well over 100 times. These two bodies of literature, the gospels plus Acts and Paul's epistles (with 12 out of 13 being cited) are recognized as inspired right there at the close of the New Testament canon, at about 100 AD.

Let's revisit the *Thomas* thesis. Why are other volumes not considered for the New Testament canon? There are really no competitors, no other gospels floating around to compete with the gospels and Acts. No other epistles have anywhere near the status of Paul's writings, with up to 200 references to all 18 of these texts right at the close of the first century. Folks, the canonical material, especially the portions that we have highlighted above, are very, very early material and recognized as authoritative.

How about *Thomas*? Clement (about 95 AD), Ignatius (107 AD), and Polycarp (110 AD) cite or refer to the gospels, Acts, and Paul many, many times. But guess what? They didn't even quote a single time from the *Gospel of Thomas*. Why?

Because they're trying to push *Thomas* away from the canon? No. There's no reason to think that *Thomas* was around during those early years. What doesn't exist cannot be quoted. If they don't know it, they cannot cite it!

On the other hand, we have plenty of evidence for the use of the authoritative New Testament gospels, Acts, and Paul's epistles. Remember: it's not the early Christians' fault if they accepted all the gospels that were in existence at the end of the first century, and there were only four of them!

PROGRAM 4 Is There a Strong Historical Basis for Believing that Jesus Rose From the Dead?

Ankerberg: Welcome. Today we're going to examine three things. First, how has modern scholarship changed its ideas about Jesus as it has examined his life? Is there still a strong historical basis for believing Jesus claimed to be God and rose from the dead? Second, we're going to talk about the main question that is in the background of all historical study about Jesus, namely, what about the miracles found in the New Testament? Can a twentieth-century historian conclude that they really happened?

Then third, we're going to look at 12 historical facts that are accepted by virtually all critical scholars today that present a solid foundational basis for believing Jesus lived, claimed to be God, died on a cross, and rose again.

But first, how has modern scholarship changed its ideas about Jesus as they have examined his life? Dr. Gary Habermas explains:

Habermas: Primarily, New Testament scholars speak today of three periods in which the investigation of the Historical Jesus flourished to one extent or another, plus a "No Quest" period thrown in for good measure. (1) Let's overview the classical period. Now there were some forerunners here, but they were not very influential. I'm talking about English deists like Thomas Woolston and Peter Annet, along with German rationalists like Herman Samuel Reimarus. But the prototypical "Lives of Jesus" were written during the period called "Old Liberalism," or "German Liberalism." Oftentimes this movement reflects the philosophical side of German idealism as it made its way into theology. For over one hundred years, many

58

scholars wrote their own, usually quite lengthy, lives of Jesus. In fact, a lot of these books had that same title: *Life of Jesus.*

In general, the usual German Liberal presupposition was that we can basically use the gospels more-or-less as historical sources, minus two large areas. One area is the wide-ranging avoidance of dogmatic theology: the Deity of Jesus Christ, the atonement, his uniqueness, exclusivism, and so on. The other area is that of supernatural events: they usually circumvented Jesus' miracles and especially his resurrection. A few of these scholars supported certain aspects of dogmatic theology and even miracles, but these were not the majority views, especially among the most influential scholars.

So, they freely made use of the gospels, at least the portions that they thought were historical. But generally, they eschewed the dogmatic theology and the belief in actual miracles. What remains? That's called the Historical Jesus.

Now, for a little over a hundred years, this movement was termed "The Quest for Historical Jesus," after Albert Schweitzer's famous book title. This well-known, highly acclaimed volume was written in 1906 and contained a reservoir of often obscure information regarding this movement.

(2) After "The First Quest" came the initial reaction— what has frequently come to be called the "No-Quest period." Karl Barth and Rudolf Bultmann were in the limelight here, but for widely divergent reasons. In spite of broad disagreements, they agreed that, while historical events are clearly found in the New Testament texts, history did not serve as a foundation for faith. Therefore, the Historical Jesus did us very little, if any, good. Faith is

sufficient, and it is not based on history. Apologetics was viewed as an abomination.

So, there was a classical liberal period–German Liberalism, when studies of the "Life of Jesus" were the norm. The pushback followed in the form of a "No-Quest period"–featured by the influential "reigns" of Barth and Bultmann. Barth came on the scene a littler earlier, but rocked the theological world in 1918 with his famous volume, *Epistle to the Roman* at the close of World War I. Bultmann was more radical than Barth, and his 1941 essay, "New Testament and Mythology," set an agenda for what was known as demythologizing—reinterpreting early mythology in terms of its existential significance in present preaching. But to repeat, both scholars were unhappy with pursuing studies of the Historical Jesus.

(3) Then, in the 1950s, scholars such as Ernst Käsemann, Günther Bornkamm, and James Robinson–all of these former students of Bultmann--thought that some of these trends were moving a little too far in the wrong direction. In some very important publications in the 1950s, like Bornkamm's *Jesus of Nazareth*, they argued that while faith is not based on history, we do need to know some basic historical facts about Jesus or we may be doomed to let him slip into the pages of legend. So they concluded that we can a few things about the Historical Jesus, though certainly not enough for a historical reconstruction of Jesus' life. Again, like their mentor Bultmann, they still didn't think faith was based on history. This became the "Second Quest for the Historical Jesus," or what it was called at the time, "The New Quest." It was a short-lived movement.

(4) What is now being called "The Third Quest for the Historical Jesus" had some forerunners in the 1970s, but this movement blossomed in the 1980s, 1990s, and ever since. We're still seeing an outpouring of books and

articles from every theological persuasion–skeptical, left, moderate, and right. Arguably, more historical information has emerged about Jesus during this period than from any of the others, and it has continued right up until the present. The books from the Third Quest basically share in common the general, overall agreement that Jesus was very much a Jewish person, and we should study him against his Jewish background. Jewish customs, anthropology, and sociology became important areas. Jesus became once again a man of the Jewish calendar, rather than a man of the Gnostic calendar, as per Rudolf Bultmann.

This is a very basic overview of four movements: three involved historical quests for Jesus (one hundred years of German Liberalism, the "New Quest," and the almost four decades of "The Third Quest of the Historical Jesus,"), as well as the "No Quest" period, sandwiched in-between the first two of these. The Third Quest is still going strong and is arguably what is currently making the study of the historical Jesus the hottest single topic in western religious venues today.

Ankerberg: Now, what about the miracles found in the New Testament? Is it possible for a twentieth-century historian to come to the conclusion that Jesus really did perform miracles and really did rise from the dead? On this topic, Dr. Habermas is an acknowledged expert who has debated the well-known philosopher Antony Flew on this topic and written scores of scholarly publications. Listen: **Habermas:** Okay, this brings us to the question of Jesus' miracles. A few members of the First Quest might argue for some of these events, but not many. The topic was usually shelved as one of the "off-limits" portions of the gospels, except to raise natural theses in place of the supernatural elements. The Second Quest really wasn't interested in this subject. But for the Third Quest, the question of Jesus' miracles is again on the front burner at the present time.

Critical scholars usually divide miracles into three categories: healing miracles, nature miracles, and exorcisms. Generally, they think that something was really going on here, at least in the sense that Jesus healed people in some sense. The crowds agreed, as well. Regarding the exorcisms, again, something was really happening. A minimal view might be that this sort of phenomenon actually transpired, even if it was another species of psychosomatic healing. Unquestionably, it was agreed both by Jesus and his contemporaries, as well as by most critical scholars today, that Jesus really did heal the sick and relieved much psychological pain. Contemporary scholars think that either a number of these gospel scenes (or something very close to them), are at least fairly accurate and even close to what actually occurred.

The supernatural portion of the miracle is still doubted by many scholars today. However, this is not a unanimous conclusion. Responding to questions like Jesus raising Lazarus from the dead or walking on water, even skeptical scholar Marcus Borg thinks that, due to Jesus' power, authority, and other qualities, we cannot be sure exactly what he actually may have been able to accomplish.[18] Plus, the vast majority of critical scholars do think that the historical situations in the gospels, or ones very similar to them, did indeed take place.

Of course, many today will respond, "Come on! We're modern. We can't believe in miracles!" But this is an inductive, scientific world. So, where is the preponderance of facts here? If we look at the data and they look like something has occurred that has a chance to be miraculous,

---

[18] Marcus Borg, Jesus, A New Vision: Spirit, Culture, and the Life of Discipleship (San Francisco: Harper Collins, 1987), pp. 59-71.

then put the question of miracles on the back burner and at first just ask the historical question: What happened in each of these instances? What happened with the resurrection? It should at least be kept in mind that if God raised Jesus, and the evidence mentioned here looks excellent, this should at least push us in the direction of openness to these issues.

Further, what often drives us to assume that miracles don't really occur? If the answer is metaphysical or methodological Naturalism, then ask your friend how she or anyone else knows that Naturalism is true? Since this worldview cannot be proven per se, why should it be the default setting of the universe? Why should an unproven position like this one occupy a privileged position over a worldview that is supported by much evidence? I think it's about time that we question Naturalism instead of everything else around it!

Some historians will simply say that they don't have either the tools or the training to decide if an event is a miracle caused by God—that they can only work with natural facts. But where does that conclusion lead?

Follow me on this. What I am pointing to here goes something like this: I want to know if a man named Jesus of Nazareth walked and talked on the earth just prior to about 30 AD. Historians will answer, "Oh, yes—we can say that all right. Virtually nobody thinks that Jesus didn't live." (By the way, even Rudolf Bultmann proclaimed, "By no means are we at the mercy of those who doubt or deny that Jesus ever lived.")[19]

---

[19] Rudolf Bultmann, "The Study of the Synoptic Gospels," in Form Criticism: Two Essays on New Testament Research, trans. by Frederick C. Grant (New York, N.Y.: Harper and Brothers, 1962), p. 60.

Okay, well tell me next, did Jesus probably die by crucifixion? And the historian might respond, "Well, that's not a problem, either. Everyone dies and we have good historical evidence for this event, not to mention some major medical testimony here." After all, even skeptical scholars are basically unanimous that Jesus died by Roman crucifixion, as supported by some of the most concrete data in the ancient world.[20] So, it appears that we occupy pretty solid ground when we assert that Jesus lived, was crucified, and died, though we, of course, cannot argue the specific details right here.[21]

Now, when we get beyond the cross, perhaps some folks begin to get a little nervous. But let's not ask the more philosophical question, "Did God intervene and pull him out of the tomb?" Instead, let's ask an easier, historical question: "Okay, we've said that Jesus of Nazareth walked and talked in Palestine, and then was probably crucified and died on the Roman cross. Did his followers at least *believe* that he was walking around soon afterward and that he appeared to people, seeming to be just fine?" This foundation seems to encapsulate much of the crux of our historical issues.

Okay, then, what natural, historical facts do we know here regarding Jesus? (1) Historians certainly do have the tools to ascertain whether this man walked and talked in first-century Palestine. (2) Historians also definitely have the tools to say that our best data indicate that he died as a victim of Roman crucifixion. (3) And historians likewise have the tools to conclude at the very least that his early

---

[20] The testimonies of John Dominic Crossan and Marcus Borg to this fact will be presented below.

[21] For details, see Gary R. Habermas, The Historical Jesus: Ancient Evidence for the Life of Christ (Joplin, MO: College Press, 1996), pp. 69-75.

followers believed and proclaimed that they saw him alive after his crucifixion.

Note carefully that point (3) does *not* say that Jesus was raised from the dead. It simply concludes that his disciples believed that they saw him again after his death— not as a ghost or an illuminated body, but simply that they believed that they saw him again. What I'm getting at here is that historians, at the very least, have a duty to pursue a line of "earthly" facts in the direction that the data most likely point us. If strong historical arguments say that Jesus taught or did thus and so, we have to be open to that direction—to at least be willing to look at that.

On our third point, I quote from the well-known skeptical agnostic scholar, Bart Ehrman:

> Historians, of course, have no difficulty whatsoever speaking about the belief in Jesus' resurrection, since this is a matter of public record. For it is a historical fact that some of Jesus' followers came to believe that he had been raised from the dead soon after his execution.[22]

What accounts for this belief? Ehrman clearly answers that question, too: "we can say with complete certainty that some of his disciples at some later time insisted that . . . he soon appeared to them, convincing them that that he had been raised from the dead."[23]

On this subject, then, we are asking straightforward, historical questions. We asked whether there existed a man named Jesus who walked and talked in Palestine, died on

---

[22] Bart D Ehrman, Jesus: Apocalyptic Prophet of the New Millennium (Oxford: Oxford University Press, 1999), p. 231.

[23] Ehrman, Ibid., p. 230.

the cross and that some people believed that they saw him afterward? These are certainly claims that historians can get their fingers on—and we have strong data here. So as I said, let's first talk about what is knowable history. The question concerning whether any of this could be a miraculous act of God is a further philosophical issue.

Ankerberg: Now, during these programs, you have heard Dr. Habermas constantly refer to historical facts about Jesus that are accepted by the majority of critical scholars. What are some of these? I asked him to identify 12 facts that most critical scholars accept as true. Listen:

Habermas: Now, the question arises, obviously, what kind of data do we have, then? What are these "historical facts" that I keep referring to? A few people may question if we even have historical facts!

Earlier I differentiated between audiences. Evangelicals may look at the New Testament text and say, "Everything I read here is a historical fact. Credible data are all over the place. Everywhere I read, I find them because I believe that the Scriptures are inspired."

Skeptics, on the other hand, might say, "No. The New Testament is only a book of ancient literature. Some claims are clearly better than others, but there's no way that it is all history."

So, we have to address the question, which are the best-evidenced historical facts here? Most scholars will grant a list of at least twelve items surrounding the overall events towards the end of Jesus' life, including his death, burial, and the nature of the disciples' claim that they saw him alive again after his death. Actually, I have long said that there are more than just twelve of these admitted historical facts, but that's the number that I'm going to list here. The majority of critical scholars will admit virtually every one of these:

1. Jesus died by crucifixion.

2. He was buried. There's nothing strange about this fact. People die, and people are buried. (We're not even designating a particular place or kind of burial.)

3. Jesus' death caused his disciples to despair and lose hope, believing his life had ended. This is psychologically natural and understandable, for sure: how would you feel if your best friend, on whose account you had left everything in order to follow, died very suddenly and horribly?

4. Now I admit, as I likewise repeat all the time, that this next fact is not quite as widely held, but the majority of scholars still think that the tomb in which Jesus was buried was discovered to be empty just a few days later.

5. Arguably, the most crucial fact here beyond Jesus' death is that his disciples had experiences that they thought were literal appearances of the risen Jesus. In other words, they *thought* that Jesus appeared to them. I'm wording this very carefully, and it is held extraordinarily widely by scholars.

6. Because of these experiences, the disciples were transformed from doubters who were afraid to identify themselves with Jesus into bold proclaimers of his death and resurrection appearances. They were even willing to die for their faith in these gospel events.

7. This message was the center of early church preaching. Remember Paul's testimony: The events of Jesus Christ's death, burial, resurrection, and appearances were "of first importance."

8. This message was especially proclaimed in the environs of Jerusalem, the city where Jesus had died and was buried just shortly before.

9. As a result of this preaching, the church was born and grew.

10. Sunday became the primary day of worship, which is a significant fact especially for the initial Jewish believers.

11. James, who had been a skeptical unbeliever, was converted to the faith most likely when he also believed that he had seen the resurrected Jesus.

12. A few years later, Saul (Paul) was also converted by an experience which he, likewise, thought to be an appearance of the risen Jesus.

What I'm saying is that, with the exception of the empty tomb, virtually all critical scholars accept as historical the events listed here, and most of these scholars will even grant the empty tomb. If anyone wants to check some of the data or sources on this, they may find lists of critical scholars who accept these facts, as I've listed many of them in my volume, *The Historical Jesus*[24] and elsewhere. Of course, there are many additional books on these subjects by others, as well.

Now, someone might say, "Now, wait a minute. Twelve facts, that's not bad, but can we shorten this list even further? Would more skeptics express their support if we were even pickier in what we accepted here?"

Well, it was precisely for this reason that I arbitrarily reduced this list to, say, three to seven facts—somewhere within that number. If I were to reduce these data, I might list something like the following five facts: (1) Jesus died due to crucifixion. (2) His disciples had experiences that they thought were appearances of the risen Jesus. (3) Their lives were transformed because of this conviction. (4) As a result, they proclaimed this message very soon after Jesus'

---

[24] Habermas, The Historical Jesus, Chap. 7, pp. 143-170.

death, actually within weeks, as we said earlier. (5) A man named Saul of Tarsus was converted to Jesus Christ by what he also concluded was a personal appearance of the risen Jesus to him.

These are five tough facts that virtually everyone is going to grant as historical, especially the scholars who have studied this area. Here's the key: I think that we can build a case for that central proclamation of this gospel message of the death and resurrection of Jesus based on just these five facts alone.

Ankerberg: Now, these are just 12 facts that are accepted by all critical scholars.

Some skeptics would probably concede 20 or more such details. But Dr. Habermas believes you only need four to six of these facts to establish a strong historical basis for saying Jesus lived, died on a cross, and rose again from the dead. Listen as he explains:

Habermas: Now, we just finished listing five historical facts that I think are going to be admitted by the vast majority of critical scholars, folks in the middle, and even those on the left side of the aisle. We might add a couple of others here in order to make additional points: (6) The resurrection was at the very center of early Christian preaching. (7) The message was taught in Jerusalem, where their claims could be checked out. (8) The apostle James, the brother of Jesus, was another skeptic who became a follower of the Christ based on his own appearance. What do we do with this brief wealth of data?

Here's my point. It has been mentioned that some critical scholars are going to recognize a longer list of historical facts. Some skeptics might event grant 20 events. But as I said, I don't need 20. I only need 12. But some may wonder, "Can you make your case with any less than the list of 12?" To that question, I'm saying that even using just five of these, yes, I think we can make just such a case. But understand, that's an arbitrary number. Why? Because virtually nobody will hone the list down that far. But I'll reduce it rather arbitrarily to 12, and then to five, or perhaps to just a few more. Here's my contention: with these data, along with the equally-recognized items that indicate and modify each of these facts (for we will no doubt be asked for the back-up!), we have enough of a basis to say that Jesus died and that he was actually seen again afterward. We can, in a sense, have our cake and eat it too with just these facts.

Ankerberg: Now, here's the bottom line for all the information we've given you today. If you just take four to six of these accepted historical facts about Jesus' life, they can also knock out and refute all of the naturalistic theories that have been proposed to explain away the resurrection of Jesus from the dead. Additional facts show that Jesus claimed to be Deity. Instead of running from Jesus, you should run to him for forgiveness and eternal life. Dr. Habermas explains:

Habermas: Using just these four to seven Minimal Facts as confirmed by the recognized data that establish each of these, which are basically just some of what most critical scholars will grant, natural theories that propose to explain the resurrection as normal events can all be shown to fail. In other words, these historical facts address attempts that basically say, "Jesus was not raised from the dead. What really happened was _____ (fill in the blank)." So with just these approximately half-dozen facts, we can refute all those major alternative hypotheses and at the same time have the very best evidences that favor the resurrection since these are also contained right in this same list.

To repeat the two criteria, or the two prerequisites, for these Minimal Facts, (1) by far the most crucial one is that each one is individually attested by strong, additional data. (2) Precisely this factual support is the reason for the second criterion: that's why they are so well recognized, admitted, and allowed by virtually all critical scholars who focus in these areas. Remember, too, that this listing is shorter than most other lists of facts produced by critical scholars for this same time period in Jesus' life. So I'm really using less facts here than most scholars would be willing to grant. This is why the "lowest common denominator" approach also describes an angle on this method!

Could someone be willing to grant historical facts, but not the same ones that appear in my list? While that's possible, it's unlikely if it is from scholars who do their research in this field. That's because the facts I've chosen are the best-attested as well as the most-recognized ones, so they would be among the first to be endorsed or allowed.

What about the person who may come along and assert, "OK, well, I'm not going to grant *any* of your half-dozen historical facts. I'm not going to allow any of these that you've listed here. So, let's see how far you get now!" So, whether just for fun, belligerence, or actual conviction, this individual states that none of these historical facts is true. Can anything be done in such a case? What sort of rejoinder is possible?

In such a case, I would build the factual underpinning from the ground up. I'd begin with zero particulars and work through each of the half dozen pieces of data, citing the evidence on behalf of each one. I'd present the evidence for each of the statements on the list. There are reasons why these facts are allowed as historical even by so many critical scholars who actually hold that the New

Testament is an unreliable book, or they would not be recognized as such!

But also remember that just because someone states that they still reject all the facts, this by no means constitutes a refutation. Until each of the data-points for each individual fact is refuted, it is simply an assertion, and, of course, anyone can assert anything! It is done all the time! As mentioned, it could even be done strictly for the sake of belligerence or out of anger.

But once the Minimal Historical Facts are established, they can also, in turn, be utilized in order to provide the major refutations of the naturalistic theories, as well as providing the chief evidences on behalf of Jesus' resurrection.

Let's take an example here by choosing not just some straw man or a weak natural theory. Let's take the most popular naturalistic theory in the Nineteenth Century—the hallucination hypothesis, though we will necessarily be very brief in the details. Jesus died for sure, but he didn't really rise from the dead. Instead, his disciples were seeing things that were not actually there. So they produced the images of the risen Jesus in their own minds—they saw merely their own subjective images.

From the list of recognized Minimal Facts, notice that the disciples had experiences that they were convinced were actual appearances of the risen Jesus. This plus the death of Jesus are the most widely recognized facts on the list.

But (1) the exceptionally early, pre-Pauline creed cited by Paul in 1 Corinthians 15:3-7 asserts three times that these experiences occurred to groups of people (15:5, 6, 7). However, hallucinations are not contagious--they do not spread, and they do not occur to many individuals at one time. Therefore, experiences in group settings of people are powerful objections since these people would not all witness the same hallucination at once.

(2) The consensus position among New Testament scholars today is that Paul probably received this creed from the apostles Peter and James, the brother of Jesus, during his first visit to Jerusalem, usually dated at just five years after Jesus' crucifixion. These initial two problems, then, would indicate that the list of appearances, including the group sightings, probably came from the apostles themselves at a very early date, especially when the other two men had the data before Paul received them. That's precisely why Paul concluded the creed by asserting that the other apostles were teaching the same thing that he was with regard to their own resurrection appearances—he heard their testimony with his own ears (1 Corinthians 15:11)!

(3) The group appearances of Jesus that are reported in the early Acts sermon summaries[25] contribute further weight to the group nature of Jesus' appearances.

Whatever evidence might be derived from the additional group sightings also recorded in the gospel accounts would provide extra evidence gathered from establishing the appearances to the group of woman, or to any of the other appearances to the disciples as listed in those sources.

(4) Within these groups of people, many different personality types, as well as both genders, were represented, from hardheaded Peter to tender-hearted John, to (presumably) the soft-hearted Marys, along with all of the others. The different genders, personalities, times, and places involved all lengthen the odds against

---

[25] Such as those found in Acts 2:32; 3:15; 5:30-32; 10:38-43; 13:30-31.

hallucinations since these experiences are related to such factors. Not all persons are "wired" for psychological events of this nature. It's highly unlikely that, among those in the different groups, that each of these people would be precisely in just the proper frame of mind to see hallucinations.

(5) Further, the apostles were thoroughly changed by these experiences.

However, hallucinations rarely transform anyone at all. In fact, most are simply talked out of their hallucinations. I know two researchers who have done some personal study during these occasions, and they found that many of these folks changed their minds, especially when the hallucinations were of one of two sorts: when their colleagues who were nearby *either* didn't witness the same thing they did *or* when it was determined that this sort of thing doesn't happen normally. Guess what? Both of these conditions would have applied to the resurrection of Jesus—if no one else present had seen him, and because dead men don't rise anyway. A few trusted friends repeating each of these factors would probably be enough to change the testimony. But of course, that never occurred because Jesus *did* appear to groups of people after his death!

(6) I have argued often that there are many indications that Jesus' burial tomb was discovered to be empty just a short time later, even though this is not quite as widely allowed by scholars. But since hallucinations definitely do not explain this feature of the accounts, another hypothesis is necessary. This simply complicates the process here rather significantly.

(7) How do we handle the conversion of the Apostle Paul? The infamous church persecutor wouldn't be in the proper frame of mind to see a hallucination! Why would

this man want to see the resurrected Jesus? What we need is *evidence* that he had somehow changed *beforehand*.

(8) The same may be said concerning Jesus' brother, James. What would we think if our brothers were getting that kind of attention? And James was a skeptic, as critical scholars usually admit. But I doubt severely that James longed to see hallucinations of his risen brother!

These are a few of the major problems that emerge from just our shortened list of historical facts that we already recognized. This is especially significant in that hallucinations are probably the most popular naturalistic thesis ever, yet it is plagued by many significant issues, even beyond these issues.

Consider an illustration of what I'm talking about here with the Minimal Facts argument. Let's say we're surrounded by a group of people, and over on one side are the conservatives. They will grant me *all* of the facts in the New Testament.

Obviously, Jesus existed, died, and was raised from the dead. The next group doesn't grant all of the data, though they allow *most* of it. The general conclusion is that Jesus was still resurrected.

Further over on the left are the folks who explain that they will acknowledge, say, between 12 and 20 of the facts. I'll either tell them that I'm willing to work with that number, or I'll actually work with less.

But for the person who says, "I'm not going to give you any of these historical facts at all," as I mentioned earlier, I would work individually from zero to each one of them. So I'd produce the data that establish each. The bottom line is that these facts alone refute the naturalistic theories on the one hand and still provide the best evidence for the resurrection on the other.

PROGRAM 5 Twelve Historical Facts that Present a Solid Foundational Basis for Believing that Jesus Lived, Claimed to be Deity, Died on a Cross, and Rose Again

Ankerberg: A popular falsehood being promoted by the tiny percentage of liberal scholars in the Jesus Seminar, is that there is very little historical evidence available to provide a strong basis for traditional Christian beliefs about Jesus. But last week, Dr. Gary Habermas listed 12 historical facts about Jesus' life that are accepted by virtually all critical scholars and showed that the Jesus Seminar is mistaken. Today we will examine the significance of those facts. My guest, Dr. Gary Habermas, was confronted by these very facts when he was a student at Michigan State University working on his Ph.D., and they served to correct his skepticism. He talks about the persuasiveness of these facts. Listen:

Habermas: In the last program, we ended with a list of about a half-dozen "Minimal Historical Facts," reduced from the original twelve. Based on the specifics that support these facts, we can argue that Jesus died and that he appeared to his followers after his death. On the other hand, naturalistic hypotheses cannot explain these same historical facts.

Perhaps I could begin with an autobiographical note here, which might be helpful. The process of arriving at these historical facts was quite crucial in my own life. I spent ten years in a skeptical frame of mind, followed by more intermittent years of questioning beyond that. I argued with Christians, actually debating with about anyone who claimed to be sure about their religious views. It might be a Jehovah's Witness, a Mormon, a Christian Scientist, but more often, my aim was taken at those who held orthodox Christian beliefs. I repeatedly questioned these factual foundations. My repeated mantra was, "You don't have facts to back that up. That's in the gospels. You don't have data for this . . . and you don't have data for that." But I had further ways yet to go down the skeptical path. At one point, I realized that I was very close to embracing Buddhism.

Once a college student who was a Christian heard that I didn't believe in the inspiration of the Bible. He asked me if that were indeed true. I will always remember his immediate response. When I told him what he had heard was accurate, he retorted, "Man, you have seven demons in you!" Then he spun around and walked away abruptly!

All my graduate studies were taken in liberal or secular institutions. For years I wondered if there was a solid enough basis for religious belief—if there was much of a foundation beyond that of faith alone, as I suspected might be about the only approach possible. I studied various sides of the key issues, different philosophies, "holy books," and religious traditions. While the Christian belief in Jesus' resurrection seemed pretty impressive for a miracle-claim, I often wondered why I could not seem to get over my doubts on the subject.

So, the study of the Minimal Facts began for me as a private project. It was certainly not for the purposes of public proclamation. I repeatedly conjectured how much of the New Testament claims could be sustained apart from the belief in some notion of inspiration, which I did not allow as a response. If we could only believe what was well-evidenced, then what remained?

After several reductions of what we could know as historical events, I arrived at a shortened list of about a dozen facts. Could these events alone answer the objections to the naturalistic theories that challenged the belief that Christ had been raised from the dead? I kept narrowing the list until I arrived at the half-dozen or so facts that I now use, events which I concluded were solid. This was the initial birth of the Minimal Facts Argument for Jesus' resurrection, although much honing was yet to take place. But it was originally designed as a personal study to answer my own questions.

Basically, I'm employing the critical method roughly the way that contemporary scholars do, treating the material similarly, and asking, even if the Bible is no more than a book of ancient literature, what can still be ascertained? After all, it cannot be less than that--it's ancient, it's got pages, and there's words on the pages! That's pretty basic! But if by treating the New Testament as a volume of ancient literature, we can still arrive at these "Core"[26] or "Minimal Facts," as I now call them, I realized that this was quite significant. If on this basis alone, the naturalistic theories can be refuted and the strongest arguments that Jesus was raised from the dead still remained, then they were worth their weight in gold.

Ankerberg: Next, we are going to examine further some of the 12 facts. First, did Jesus actually die on a cross? In the Qur'an, Islam claims that Jesus did not die on the cross; something else happened. Further, naturalistic scholars claim that Jesus did not die on the cross, rather he just fainted or swooned. Now, the problem with these theories is that the historical facts of Jesus' death will not

---

[26] This was one of my original names for these facts.

allow such interpretations. Dr. Gary Habermas explains why. Listen:

Habermas: The very first fact on this list is that Jesus died. Why do scholars in these areas so rarely question the death of Jesus today? Why do some of the co-founders of the Jesus Seminar, for example, highly influential scholars such as Marcus Borg[27] and John Dominic Crossan,[28] both assert that the fact that Jesus died by crucifixion is the surest fact that we have from his career? Because the data are so strong.

Now, what are some of the backups for this fact? We'll give several responses here. (1) To start, the majority medical view is still that death by crucifixion is essentially death by asphyxiation. When someone hangs on a cross and the weight of his body pulls down on the intercostal, pectoral, and deltoid muscles around the lungs, the body reaches a state where the weight drags down on them, and it is increasingly impossible to exhale.

Actually, in the 1950s, an experiment was performed in Germany by a medical doctor, where male volunteers were tied to and suspended from 2-x-4s. These males lost consciousness in a maximum of 12 minutes. Now, on the cross, they could push up, in this case, on the nails. When the victim pushed up to relieve those chest muscles, they could breathe more easily. But when they could not stay up there for long and slumped down again, when they were down in the low position on the cross, they began

---

[27] Borg, *Jesus, A New Vision*, 179.

[28] 28 John Dominic Crossan states, "Jesus' death by execution under Pontius Pilate is as sure as anything historical can ever be" (5) (*Who Killed Jesus? Exposing the Roots of Anti-Semitism in the Gospel Story of the Death of Jesus* [San Francisco: Harper Collins, 1995], 5. Cf. also Crossan's *Jesus: A Revolutionary Biography* (San Francisco: Harper Collins, 1994), 145.)

asphyxiating all over again. So, a Roman soldier at the cross did not have to have a medical degree. If the victim was hanging low on the cross for any amount of time, let's say 30 minutes, then he's dead.

(2) Further, we're told in the literature that additional death blows were often administered to crucifixion victims in order to insure their deaths. But when they saw that Jesus was already dead (probably because he had been hanging in the low position for some time), we are told that they stabbed him in the chest, from which blood and water flowed out. By far the most common medical view on the blood and water is that the pericardial sac around the heart ("water") plus the heart (the blood) had been pierced, insuring death. The act of such a final *coup de grace* is confirmed from extra-biblical, non-Christian accounts, including this very act of piercing the chest in order to confirm death.

In the ancient crucifixion accounts, there are a number of accounts of a *coup de grace*, a crushing blow, that's done at the end of crucifixion to end the execution. We have an account of a man whose skull was crushed to finish the process; another man was threatened with a bow and arrow. As mentioned, we have other cases besides Jesus' where the victim was stabbed in order to make sure that he was dead. Then there's what's known as *crucifragium* in Latin, the breaking of the ankles so the person cannot push back up again, causing final asphyxiation. In all of these cases, the executioner is basically showing everyone that this person is not walking away alive during his watch.

So the first two reasons include asphyxiation from hanging low on the cross, which cannot be faked. The second is the soldier's deathblow, which in Jesus' case consisted of the spear wound into the chest and heart. In a medical article published in the *Journal of the American*

Medical Association some 15 years ago, the decision was that Jesus' death resulted primarily from asphyxiation. The researchers included a Mayo Clinic pathologist, and they confirmed that the spear entered Jesus' heart.

Again, the water came from the pericardial sac surrounding the heart and the blood from the heart itself. The conclusion was that the blow ensured that Jesus had already died.[29]

(3) Now, a little more gore comes from a condition popularly called "sucking chest." It's a very well-known medical phenomenon, and it occurs when someone is stabbed or otherwise pierced through the upper thoracic area. In a living person, this action produces a sucking sound from that wound. Such a sound sounds exactly as if the victim is still breathing, though that is not exactly what is happening in such a case. A hunter told me just today that when he shot a deer once through the chest, he walked up to it and heard such a noise. So, naturally, he shot the animal once again to make sure, and the noise stopped because the animal died. The point here is that such a response would be a normal action to ensure death—just as would have been the case with Jesus and the soldiers. If Jesus was stabbed in the chest and he was still alive, the sucking chest syndrome would cause another finishing blow.

These are some of the reasons for holding that crucifixion was lethal and included built-in checks and balances for assurance. The medical nature of asphyxiation, the heart wound, and potentially the sucking chest condition are all very serious objections.

---

[29] 29 William D. Edwards, Wesley J. Gabel, and Floyd E. Hosmer, "On the Physical Death of Jesus Christ," *Journal of the American Medical Association*, vol. 255 (21 March 1986).

However, none of these responses was the chief reason for the failure of the swoon theory, as it lost its popularity back in the days of Nineteenth-Century German Liberalism. Borg, Crossan, and the JAMA article, plus the vast majority of critical scholars today, all attest to its failure. But back in 1864, a German Liberal scholar named David Strauss updated his earlier *Life of Jesus*. Strauss was so liberal that he had been dismissed from the leading liberal German university at that time, Tübingen. He was pensioned off for life because of his highly critical views. Yet, his infamous critique of the apparent death hypothesis remains even at present, the most influential reason for dismissing this hypothesis, which, by the way, was the most popular natural theory up until about 1835.

Expanding his thoughts, here's what Strauss asserted: The main problem with the swoon theory is the logic as much or more than it was the medical issues. It's basically self-contradictory. Let's check out his reasons: Jesus should have died on the cross, but he did not. Don't worry about it. He should have died in the tomb without medical help. No problem. Assuming a burial in a tomb, he couldn't have rolled the stone away in his physical condition. That took several men, and he'd be rolling the stone uphill out of the little gully in front of the tomb in his severely weakened condition. But don't bother--he rolled the stone away anyway. How far did he walk? I don't know; perhaps he traveled a quarter of a mile, at least, to where the disciples were hiding, walking on feet that were pierced by nails for hours.

As Strauss pointed out, these are not the main issues. The chief problem with postulating that Jesus didn't die by crucifixion occurs when Jesus arrives at the residence where the disciples were staying and knocks on the door. What are his followers going to see? What will Jesus look like? He's pale. He's sweating. The side wound has opened up again, and he is bleeding. He's hunched over, limping severely, and clearly in much pain. He has not even washed his hair—sweat and blood are caked in it. Then he delivers his surprise message, rather haltingly: "Fellows . . . I told you . . . that I would . . . rise again from the dead."

What happens next? Jesus is alive, for sure. But was he raised in a new body? Decidedly, No! Peter might start barking out orders: "Someone get the Lord a chair. Andrew, go get some warm water and a cloth—these wounds must be cleaned immediately. John, go get the doctor and tell him it's an emergency." His disciples would probably even exclaim, "Thank the Lord, he has been spared," or perhaps just simply, "He's alive!" But they wouldn't say, "Thank the Lord, he's been raised from the dead in a new body!" That's precisely what the term "resurrection" meant. So don't expect to see Phillip over in the corner, saying, as the New Testament teaches often, "Oh boy! Someday I'm going to have a new resurrection body just like Jesus' body!" No thanks--I think I will keep the body I have right now!

Now, this is precisely Strauss' point. The swoon theory teaches something that we often miss here: Jesus would be *alive*, indeed, for at least a little while, but he most certainly would *not be raised* from the dead! That's quite clear. So, what's the main problem here? If the disciples didn't at least believe that he was raised, they would have no cause to teach the New Testament message of the Good News of the gospel message! Hence, even as Paul states, there would be no church, no cause even for preaching, no forgiveness, no eternal hope in Jesus. The disciples would, at the very least, have to *believe* that Jesus had been raised. The swoon theory doesn't even give us that truth—in fact, it is diametrically opposed to it! So it cannot even get off the ground in the first place.

(5) Lastly, we have many multiple and independent historical sources for Jesus' death by crucifixion—at least a dozen. It is the most-reported event from non-New Testament sources, including well-known non-Christian historians such as Josephus, Tacitus, the Syrian Lucian, along with others.

In conclusion, asphyxiation, the heart wound, sucking chest, Strauss' critique in particular, and a wealth of independent historical sources is more than we need. But other problems remain for this theory, too. (6) What do critics do with Paul's conversion, specifically on this view? (7) How do they explain James' conversion? How were these two apostles convinced to join the early church crowd here, given this response? The conclusion assuredly is that Jesus died on the cross due to Roman crucifixion.

Ankerberg: Now, I also asked Dr. Habermas to say a word about Hugh Schonfeld's book, *The Passover Plot*, which claims Jesus was given drugs while on the cross and just appeared to die. Here's Dr. Habermas' response:

Habermas: Now, what happens when we apply this critique of the apparent death theory to a book like the 1965 bestseller, *The Passover Plot*? The author suggested that Jesus did not die on the cross. By the way, a lot of people don't remember this, but Schonfield remarked that this view was only a suggestion—he did not assert that this really had to be what happened. In fact, he considers and even notes other possible but natural hypotheses of what may have occurred![30]

But Schonfield favored the view that Jesus may not have died on the cross. Well, his view would have to explain all of the historical and medical hurdles just

---

[30] 30 Hugh J. Schonfield, *The Passover Plot: A New Interpretation of the Life and Death of Jesus* (New York, N.Y.: Bantam, 1967), pp. 165-173.

mentioned here—asphyxiation, the heart wound (which he seems to accept, even stating that it would make Jesus' chances for survival "very slender"!).[31] What about the sucking chest? But most of all, he would have to explain Strauss' famous critique. And then there are still all the many independent, even non-Christian historical sources that oppose his view.

So as one might expect, the swoon theory of *The Passover Plot* sold many copies, but it was largely ignored even by critical scholars. In fact, it appeared in critiques by scholars who basically wanted to distance themselves from such writings, reminding their readers that we cannot rule out material in this manner.[32]

In fact, after David Strauss' critique in 1864, Albert Schweitzer's famous book on *The Quest of the Historical Jesus* lists no scholars who came up with the swoon theory after 1840. Historically speaking, if you pardon the pun, Strauss' critique killed the swoon theory.

Ankerberg: Dr. Gary Habermas is laying out 12 historical facts that are accepted by virtually all critical scholars today. The importance of these 12 facts is that they form a solid historical foundation for traditional Christian beliefs about Jesus, they repudiate the Jesus Seminar, and shoot down all naturalistic explanations which have attempted to explain away Jesus' resurrection. The next fact we're going to look at is that Jesus was buried. Why is that so important? Listen:

---

[31] 31 Ibid, p. 165.

[32] 32 One example is by well-known New Testament critical scholar John A.T. Robinson who lists this text as an example of one "that anywhere else would be laughed out of court." (Robinson, *Can We Trust the New Testament?* [Grand Rapids, MI: Eerdmans, 1977], pp. 14-16.)

Habermas: For the Christian believer for whom the death and resurrection of Jesus are crucially important, as Paul mentions its being "of first importance," where do we go next? Jesus died on the cross, as many non-Christian writings attest, including, apparently, the Jewish Talmud. And then we're told, "He was buried." Now, this is often not questioned--it's a pretty normal event: people who die get buried. But what facts do we have at our disposal in favor of the burial accounts, as we learn of them in the New Testament?

(1) Although today critics are not so inclined to take the gospels as well as they accept at least Paul's "uncontested" epistles, let's begin with the comment that just because a critic doesn't necessarily like the gospels, that does not somehow whisk or otherwise automatically explain them away.

(2) Although other suggestions besides Joseph's tomb have been favored by some scholars as Jesus' resting place, where is the actual evidence that Jesus was buried somewhere else? That's the key. Where are the *facts* indicating that he was buried in another location? I'm not so much asking for potential options here ("Maybe this . . . , perhaps that . . . ."), but where is the *actual evidence* that another scenario is precisely what happened to Jesus? Let's ask the critical scholar the same question in reverse that they request of Christians: where's your data to show that Jesus wasn't buried just like the gospels stated?

(3) All four gospels agree both regarding the tomb where Jesus was buried, as well as its being empty. A lot of scholars have also made the point that Joseph of Arimathea and Nicodemus were not exactly household names in the early church to mention in these burial accounts unless they were the fellows who actually buried Jesus. Why dredge up these names out of obscurity if so little mileage is gained from the exercise, especially if they

weren't really the people anyway? It makes more sense that they were the ones who actually performed the burial process.

(4) Continuing, we have a few exceptionally early texts that we've mentioned before, such as 1 Corinthians 15:3-4, which is probably the earliest and declares the conclusion clearly that Jesus' was buried. The pre-Pauline creed repeats that, "He died for our sins according to the scriptures, and that he was buried, and that he was raised again the third day, and that he appeared." [1 Cor. 15:3-5] Now, what follows from that sequence in this very early, pre-Pauline text? If somebody is dead, then buried, then raised, and then appeared, the strong implication is that the one who went down in burial is the same one who came up in order to appear. Paul does not doubt that there was a burial, but he's going to go further than that to the empty tomb. But if we stop precisely at the burial, that's some very specific, early evidence.

(5) Another early consideration is drawn from the early sermon summaries such as Acts 2:29-32 (which is Petrine) and Acts 13:29 (which is Pauline), both of which contrast the corruption that occurred to David's body with what did *not* happen to Jesus' body after his burial. As I mentioned above, critical scholars often grant that these summaries contain the abbreviated theology that marks them as early preaching synopses, and here they teach a burial in a verifiable location.

We might list briefly several other pointers to the traditional accounts of Jesus' burial, like (6) Jerusalem being the very last place that any Christian should ever want to publicly proclaim Jesus' burial if he had not been buried there. It was the only location in the ancient world where the claim could so readily be refuted, perhaps after a walk of just an hour or so. Thus, the city of Jerusalem is a horrible place to preach if Jesus actually had not been interred there.

(7) It was quite likely that the Jewish leaders would be concerned about not losing track of Jesus' body, both since they had tried for such a long time to silence him and because losing his body would be too close to the disciples gaining a step up in being able to proclaim that he had been raised from the dead. Besides, the Jewish polemic that the disciples stole Jesus' dead body (Matt. 28:11-14) supports both their profound interest in the question, as well as their acknowledging the traditional place of his burial!

(8) If the Roman soldiers were the ones who had buried his body, they could hardly have forgotten where anyone at all was buried in the space of just a few days, let alone someone of Jesus' stature. Besides, Pilate might have asked them for the details, especially given his questioning the centurion regarding the truth of Jesus' death (Mk. 15:44-45).

(9) Perhaps even most recent scholars maintain the likelihood that Mark employed an earlier source for his passion and burial accounts. This source would itself confirm further Joseph's traditional burial site.

(10) Although the women witnesses are usually considered to be the best evidence for the empty tomb, their trip to the stone sepulcher with spices to finish the burial process strongly supports the traditional burial. There was no question in their minds that they were going to the right burial cave.

So, there are some early creedal/sermonic texts that record Jesus' burial. We've got the unanimous gospel testimony, plus the likely pre-Markan source as further attestation. Both the location of Jerusalem and the female testimony, plus several additional arguments, all support the traditional account of Jesus' burial taught by the gospels. Especially when we consider that no actual evidence places Jesus' body elsewhere, these are very strong considerations favoring Jesus' burial in Joseph of Arimathea's private family burial cave.

Ankerberg: The next fact we want to look at is the empty tomb. This, too, is a fact of history, and it leads to the question: What happened to Jesus' body? Dr. Habermas explains:

Habermas: Okay, then, let's move on to the next step. Jesus died. He was buried. Afterward, what happened in that tomb? Well, the Christian account is that he was raised from the dead, but in-between his burial and his resurrection, he left an empty tomb behind. Are there any reasons to believe that?

I think that the first point to be made here is that the burial and empty tomb accounts are almost always flip sides of the same coin. Thus, all ten of the arguments just enumerated above, except for (8) regarding the Roman soldiers, extend the traditional burial accounts in the tomb belonging to Joseph to that same sepulcher being empty very quickly afterward. However, we will employ a different order than the list we just gave above.

(1-3) Again, the initial set of three points above concerned all four gospels recording their accounts that Jesus' burial tomb was discovered to be empty. This point of multiple source attestation is a strong one. On the other hand, no specific sources claim that Jesus' body was actually buried elsewhere. The gospel testimony here needs to be disproven in order for it not to count. Only fairly radical to radical critical scholars would tend to avoid the gospels most of the time. Moderate scholars, for example, use gospel passages carefully, but fairly widely.

The traditional burial and the empty tomb scenarios definitely begin with the best case.

(4-5) At least two other evidences should be considered at least as strong as this unanimous gospel testimony: as we've often said now, the earliest witnesses to the empty tomb were reportedly women. Why is that so crucial? Because if you're making up a story by placing different words back into the mouths of Jesus and the earliest Christians sometime later, such as our Monday morning quarterbacking scenario, you would dare not use the women as your star witnesses. They should not be the first line of defense.

Why were they used unanimously, then? In the first century Mediterranean area, women were generally allowed to testify in a court of law, but inversely to the importance of the testimony needed. They were not thought to be able, to tell the truth, as we are actually told in the literature. So they shouldn't testify regarding crucially important matters. So why do we utilize folks who are doubtfully helpful for the witness stand? It might be similar to making little children our chief witnesses. Question: the bottom line is, why would we ever allow witnesses to take the stand when they are considered less than the best? Answer: When they are still the best and/or the only witnesses.

The other reason of the two in this category is this: again, as with the burial, so with the open tomb, the city of Jerusalem is the very last place to proclaim the empty tomb if it were false, because a mere afternoon or evening walk could disprove it. Even if the body were still there but too decomposed to be recognized, the chief point here is that the early New Testament proclamation was not that there was a body in the tomb but that we don't know the identity. The message was that the tomb was *empty*— meaning that *no one* was buried there.

(6) Probably the next strongest argument for the empty tomb is not one of the reasons above for Jesus' burial. It has been quite well established for the last few decades[33] that for Jews, the resurrection of the dead was a bodily event—bodies were raised from the dead. So if a dead body were buried and rose again, it would rise in a bodily manner.

(7-9) Some very early texts, such as the pre-Pauline creedal passage in 1 Corinthians 15:3-5, for Jews, required that if Jesus died for our sins, was buried, was raised, and appeared to his followers, it would be a bodily event and so the tomb would have been empty. So when the same person is buried and then raised, what emerges is a body. What's gone down has come up. There is a strong implication here in 1 Corinthians 15 that requires an empty tomb.

The early sermon summaries in Acts 2:29-32 and Acts 13:29 are additional texts that more specifically report that, unlike David, Jesus was buried but did not remain in the tomb. That Jesus' body did not decompose, as David's did, indicated that the sepulcher was empty.

And if, as we mentioned above, recent scholars largely maintain the likelihood that Mark employed an earlier source for his passion and burial accounts, then this source would confirm both the traditional burial as well as the empty tomb, just as Mark reports.

(10) Once again, it must be considered highly likely that the Jewish leaders would be concerned about

---

[33] 33 An excellent example is argued clearly by Robert Gundry, in *Sōma in Biblical Theology, with Emphasis on Pauline Anthropology* (Cambridge: Cambridge University Press, 1976; Grand Rapids, MI: Zondervan, Academie [sic] Books, 1987). See especially chapter 13, "The *Sōma* in Death and Resurrection," pp. 159-183.

knowing exactly where Jesus' body was buried, both since they wanted to be sure that this time they were finally going to silence him and because losing track of his body could potentially be to allow the disciples to proclaim that Jesus had been raised from the dead.

We have already mentioned the Jewish polemic that the disciples stole Jesus' dead body (Matt. 28:11-14). Both Justin Martyr (*Dialogue with Trypho* 108) and Tertullian (*On Spectacles* 30) assert that this continued to be the Jewish contention around the Mediterranean world until at least 200 AD. If these accusations were in fact, the Jewish claims, then this serves as enemy attestation that Jesus' tomb was empty.

True, the Jewish leaders taught that the disciples stole Jesus' body, though scarcely any major scholar has held that thesis for well over 200 years. Some of the chief reasons for this dismissal, even among critical scholars, is that liars who know that they are lying tend not to make good martyrs. Further, the disciples' life-long transformations and their honest beliefs are also huge issues. Neither do we have adequate explanations for the conversions of James, the brother of Jesus, or for Paul.

So that explanation does not make a lot of sense. But what remains? If the disciples did not steal Jesus' body, what we are left with is an empty tomb. So, it seems, rather, that the Jewish leaders were simply fabricating an explanation in order to try to explain the unexplained historical fact that Jesus' dead body was missing. So, here's ten arguments favoring the historicity of the empty tomb, though literally twice that many could have been listed. This historical fact is simply that strong. The female testimony, the proclamation in the city of Jerusalem where the claim could have been either verified or falsified, and the multiple source attestation, in my estimation, are the strongest three arguments here, though there are certainly other good ones, as well.

Ankerberg: Now, we've looked at three historical facts about Jesus today: that he did die from crucifixion; he was buried, and his tomb was empty. Next week we will examine the fact that all of Jesus' disciples *believed* that Jesus had appeared to them after they had seen him crucified and buried. What explains this fact? Group hallucinations, visions? Or that Jesus really appeared? We'll answer those questions next week. But now Dr. Habermas summarizes what we've seen today and its importance to you:

Habermas: Where are we going with all this? First, critical scholars will grant at least a dozen or two historical facts at the end of Jesus' life on earth. We only used twelve of these. For those who may think that twelve is too many, believe me, that's very few allowed by the published authors who deal with these subjects. But then we cut that list down rather arbitrarily to about a half-dozen of these. We argued that, on that basis alone, the Jesus Christ who died by crucifixion was the same person who was raised from the dead. These two events were sandwiched around a burial and an empty tomb. We provided ten reasons for accepting the historicity of each of these historical events.

The thing we have not said much about yet is Jesus' post-resurrection appearances. What is the chief evidence for these historical events? The critical community is willing to admit that Jesus' disciples had experiences that they really thought were appearances of the risen Jesus. This is the best evidence for the resurrection, as we'll see.

PROGRAM 6 One of the Most Controversial Facts of Jesus' Life--His Appearing to His Disciples After his Death

Ankerberg: Welcome. In the last few weeks Dr. Gary Habermas has been presenting and documenting 12 historical facts that virtually all critical scholars today believe about Jesus. He has gone even further and stated that if you accept just a half dozen of these acknowledged facts, they will provide you with a solid, historical foundation for believing in the traditional view of Jesus. Today we will examine one of the most controversial facts of Jesus' life: his appearing to his disciples. This evidence confronted Dr. Habermas during his skeptical days, working on his Ph.D. at Michigan State University. Listen:

Habermas: Last week I made the comment that I spent 10 years in more of a skeptical mode, followed by more sporadic doubts for years after that. I argued with Christians, especially regarding their basis for believing what they did about Scripture.

I would respond: "But you can't know this," and "You can't know that." I would also accuse them of just quoting Scripture passages to me. But I couldn't get rid of certain facts from my own research. I ended up doing my Ph.D. at Michigan State University, and my dissertation topic was the historicity of the resurrection of Jesus. Several of my professors didn't agree with where I was heading, and I imagine that they were not very excited about my proposal. But they never said so, and they were very fair about it. As nearly as I could tell, two of my committee members were agnostics (one of those a Jewish scholar) and a third one was a skeptic. The skeptic told me after I received the committee's approval, "Just don't say that the resurrection happened because the Bible said so."

I would never have argued like that anyway because that wasn't my view. So, it came down to the historical facts that evidenced this event and whether or not it could be said that the resurrection was a historical fact.

We need to make one absolutely crucial note before moving on: when my professor told me not to say that the resurrection happened because the New Testament said so, neither he nor other critical scholars meant that the New Testament could never be cited at all. Christians seem to think quite frequently that this is what critics mean, but that is not the case at all. This is more than clear since skeptics will almost always cite the relevant biblical texts when speaking on this topic, even if conservative scholars do not!

What he meant was, various passages could definitely be utilized, but only in cases where these were critically-attested passages, that is, the texts that were established according to critical standards. Believers often call this the "pick-and-choose" method, but critical scholars are usually very specific with regard to why particular passages are acceptable. These Scripture portions need to meet particular historical standards. Often, these same or similar standards are also applied to other ancient works.

Now then, how should we treat the New Testament accounts of the resurrection appearances? We can begin precisely where critical scholars do since virtually every one of them will admit and allow that the disciples had real experiences of some sort that convinced them that they had witnessed real appearances of the risen Jesus. It is generally recognized that these experiences and beliefs on their part were indisputable facts from the New Testament. Otherwise, many things that we know to be true could not be explained unless the disciples at least *believed* that they had seen the risen Jesus.

Why is this historical fact conceded? There are actually several reasons for this conclusion. For example, we have their reports, as we have already pointed out in detail. Were these things reported truthfully? For starters, it is usually recognized that when someone willingly gives their life for a cause, be it willingly dying for one's country such as kamikaze pilots in World War II, or for an ideology, even a non-Christian one; we generally acknowledge that whether or not they were mistaken, they really believed what they died for. That's the key each time. Nothing else adequately explains very well their actions, beliefs, and overall mindset. They believed their country, philosophy, or religious views were worth dying for.

Even critical scholars rightly extend that same conclusion to Jesus' disciples. The best explanation by far is that they believed that Jesus was actually raised from the dead. No less a skeptic than Rudolf Bultmann himself, in his seminal essay on demythologization, "New Testament and Mythology," determined that even secular historians would allow that Jesus' earliest followers believed that they saw the risen Jesus, referring to it as a historical fact. That's definitely the major fact here, and it is one that is freely admitted and allowed. Everything else flows from there to the actual post-death appearances of Jesus.

Ankerberg: Next, you're probably saying, "I agree that it's an indisputable fact that the disciples believed they saw Jesus, but the question is how we can get from, "they thought they saw the risen Jesus" to "they actually saw him"? In his own skeptical days, Dr. Habermas had to wrestle with this question himself. Here's what he discovered.

Habermas: Now, as Dr. Ankerberg just said, I imagine many folks who are listening might say, "Fine, I'll grant you that the disciples *believed* that they saw the risen Jesus—they *thought* that they saw him. But people believe they saw all sorts of things and are clearly mistaken. So how in the world do you get from 'they thought they saw him' to 'they really did see him'?"

Initially, recall those half dozen "Minimal Facts" that we listed and discussed in some detail, that are so well-evidenced and acknowledged as historical by virtually all critical scholars. Using these, there are several additional reasons here that point clearly to the fact that the disciples actually did see the risen Jesus. Not only was this reported by the very folks who thought they saw him when Paul interviewed them more than once, but this message was formalized very, very early in the pre-Pauline creeds and the Acts sermon summaries.

Further, their lives were changed thoroughly, to the point that they were willing to die for their faith (and early sources attest that many actually did so). Recall here that the resurrection was their central proclamation, as well— their foundational point -- hence, it was this specific belief that they were the most sure of and were the most willing to die for. It was the gospel, Paul attests, "as of first importance." Then how do we get Paul the persecutor onboard except due to his thinking that he also saw the risen Jesus, as well? The exact same thing is true for James the skeptic, too. They were completely on board and died for this same belief. How do all of these things happen? So that every one of these witnesses agreed that they saw the risen Jesus as the center of their faith, and were willing to die for this belief, indicated that they *really* believed it!

So, I get it—anyone can "see" about anything. We know that—so we checked out those options, too. Here we need to remember my earlier comments that the longer list of twelve and especially the half-dozen historical facts in particular, along with the data that support these Minimal Facts, are enough to enumerate the major reasons why the key naturalistic theories fail to explain these facts other than by the resurrection. We even briefly explored some major natural options. Okay, so the disciples thought that they saw the risen Jesus, but some people simply say that they saw hallucinations. But we also pointed out in some detail how hallucinations are clearly unable to explain the appearances.

So then other "what if" scenarios may be attempted, too, such as, "That's because they really did see him! Jesus never died in the first place, so he just showed up a little while later." However, that clearly did not work, either, as we detailed briefly above. These are only some alternative examples, although they are major ones. In a similar way, all the naturalistic theories fail, and that's more than just a statement. I have written about these alternative options and their problems in great detail, in hundreds of pages, in fact.

What does Christianity have that no other religion does? Other major founders were believed to be messiahs or prophets of one sort or another, too. Anybody can be wrong about these things, as well. However, there was something different about Jesus' disciples. They didn't just say that Jesus was the Messiah, but that his resurrection from the dead was the evidence for it. Jesus had already said that earlier, too! And here's another one of the keys: *The disciples were the only persons in history who were in the position to know whether or not they really saw someone who had been raised from the dead.* No other founder of any other belief system qualifies on this score because there is no evidence that anyone else ever rose from the dead! The disciples' central claim was, "We saw him after he died." That's unique in the history of religions. That's why Paul was so sure that he declared after just repeating a list of the appearances, that, "If Christ has not been raised from the dead," then our faith is vain." [1 Cor. 15:14]

Now, let me tell a little story that might help to drive home a few of these points. Let's talk about a very common human experience, say, shopping at the grocery store. Let's say we both went separately to the store, and I saw you there last night. I might recall a conversation we had, and I reminded you of it: "Remember, we were talking about how to grill that steak?" Now, say that several of our buddies also happened to be there in a small group and we kept running into them throughout the store.

Once, several of us spoke with you. Another time, it was just me. Rounding another corner, five of us were all close and gathered around. Now let's say for a more parallel case here, there were several such occasions over a month-long period of time one summer. Once, eleven or twelve of us all saw you in a different store. Now, it would be pretty hard for someone to claim that we never saw you in these places. That would especially be the case if the other fellows confirmed the stories, in groups of twos and threes, or even as a larger group. For now, I'll leave the story right here.

The disciples claimed further that "I believe his claims that he is the Son of God. I believe that God vindicated him as well as his teachings by raising him." We have said that others have claimed that certain folks were prophets and so on. However, Jesus' disciples included something additional: "I saw you after you died. I touched you. And I wasn't the only one there, either." Parts of these times were rather ordinary experiences. "True, when you first appeared, I was shocked. But once that part was over, we all shared pretty normal times together." The gospels report some of these things: Jesus walked around, he talked, and he even cooked a shore lunch. He did regular things, as in the grocery store example.

Now, as mentioned, several of us saw you both singly and in small groups in the grocery store last night, as well as other times and places throughout that summer. But here's the "catch": what if all of us also had been present at your funeral just a few days beforehand? What if several of us saw your body in the casket, and we saw one or two of your family members even reach over and touch you, confirming that you were indeed dead? *Then* came tonight, and we all saw you in the store? Now what? Many of your buddies saw you there together, too, and needless to say, we were stunned!

Now here's the next question: how much evidence would it take to convince all of us that it was really you present in that store? What about convincing somebody else who was not there that we all saw you there a few days after your funeral? The point is, we could be convinced of two things: you were absolutely dead when we saw you last. And we also know that we all saw you in the store, walking around, smiling, and talking with us, even though we don't know exactly how to explain it. But the circumstances were too easily noticeable to miss: like everyone else, we saw you picking up food. We saw you doing quite normal sorts of things. We even shook hands with you (several times!), and we couldn't help but notice that the wounds from the car accident that killed you were all perfectly healed, too.

My point is that the disciples didn't just say, "I believe that Jesus was a special individual." They said something much more radical: "We saw Jesus alive again after he died in a pretty gruesome manner." Somehow, we have to do justice to their confirmed statements that they had *actually seen him again* afterward. The resurrection would have been miraculous. However, once that occurred, the walking, talking, smiling, and the shore lunch were pretty much normal events.

Now, let's go back to our story. Seeing you in the grocery store was quite normal, as well. We did, in fact, see you there last week. I'm absolutely positive of that, and you know what? I'll remember that for the rest of my life. Every time I wonder about it, I'll check it out with my buddies. "We saw him there" was the unanimous verdict. I think that's what we're dealing with here. Yes, the disciples believed that Jesus was the Messiah, and they believed that he was raised from the dead. But besides that, they've got an additional punch here that nobody else has: what we might call the "We all saw you in the grocery store" scenario. If my faith is based on my seeing you at the store, I'm telling you, it's pretty firm. After all, that's what the disciples said as well: They saw the risen Jesus, and seeing is believing. Tell me: what else could the disciples have done?

Ankerberg: Now, 250 years ago, in his famous essay against the belief in miracles, David Hume said that people don't accept miracles because "the preponderance of evidence outweighs such events." That is, we've all had a lot of experience that has led us to the conclusion that people who die don't come back to life again. But what new evidence could make us change our minds? Was this new exceptional evidence given to Jesus' disciples? Dr. Gary Habermas says, yes. Listen:

Habermas: I think that I would initially raise some problems with David Hume's thesis itself. In the last couple of decades, the preponderance of studies specifically on his miracles essay have gone against him. He's been criticized for several key, largely theoretical issues: a priori dismissals of evidenced data, totally misconstruing the nature of the inductive method and how data are gathered, not realizing that the answer to God's existence could easily solve the miracles issue by itself (especially when other recent studies have shown that Hume himself was possibly if not probably a theist of some variety), and so on.

But back to the story that I have been developing here, I could be quite convinced, especially of some largely mundane events such as my seeing you at the grocery store. But I am also equally positive that you were dead, as well, which may have been something like the process that the disciples went through. There are two main questions here—was Jesus actually dead? If that is answered positively, then did we all really, truly see him afterward?

We might even be satisfied to leave it right there if I am positive of the answers to these two questions: that you died in an accident because I was at your funeral and remember well those bad scars, and if we were equally positive that several of us saw you alive again, healed scars and all, at the store and elsewhere. But because we are a potentially skeptical lot, we must go what may seem to us to be beyond the call of duty: Was this all a joke of some sort? Did you have a twin (with the same scars!)? Could it have been a hallucination?

But as we tick off the reasons against these "What if" scenarios in the case of Jesus, it might occur to us that we already have enough data here, especially when it is combined with Jesus' overall world view (his claims to Deity, predicting his own death and resurrection, healing people regularly, and so on), to undergo a shift in thinking! He must have been raised from the dead!

Here's my overall point about the state of the evidence. David Hume argued otherwise about 250 years ago, but in certain circumstances, we might know that supernatural events have actually occurred. In this case, we have many arguments that this man was raised from the dead. How would I know that? Such a shift in thinking could come due to the preponderance of the positive data--by an overwhelming piling up of the positive reasons. After all, what is so bad about a supernatural world view? Jesus Christ definitely held such a position, he was dead, and we definitely saw him again later, alive. It's a theological version of 1 + 1 = 2!

Therefore, David Hume's general point that dead men don't rise may be overridden in a very particular circumstance. Why? Because we have plenty of evidence that this man was dead three days ago, and today we have at least that much evidence, if not more, that he was seen again, alive. But then the evidence grew as both singly, and in groups, more people also witnessed him alive. Facts can add up like that until sometimes we just have to throw out hypotheses that say that these things cannot ever happen.

Now, going back to those half-dozen historical facts, what do we have here that indicates that Jesus was raised from the dead? Well, he was dead, asphyxiated, probably stabbed in the heart, without a sucking chest. To turn Strauss another way, coming back in anything but a raised body wouldn't convince anybody of a resurrection anyway.

Then we have witnesses who keep saying, "I saw the risen Jesus." This happened to individuals and groups alike.

Two of those who saw him included this person named Paul, on his way to kill and imprison Christians. He's not in the mood to see the resurrected Jesus. Then, boom--Jesus is standing right there in front of him. Paul attested twice in 1 Corinthians that he had seen the risen Jesus. These events also included James, the insider, the family skeptic, who likewise met his risen brother.

Then their lives were transformed, not because of his teachings alone or due to some general euphoria, but because this event corroborated Jesus' world view, as just mentioned. That means that God the Father of Jesus, was involved and raised his Son in order to corroborate the truth of Jesus' teachings. Therefore, with the presence of God's actions, the event may be proclaimed as a miracle. Precisely because of the resurrection, the disciples' faith was anything but vain. Now we can say that that also describes us today!

At each of these points, I'm saying that the inductive probabilities pile up further and further. The general rule that dead men don't rise is looking less and less likely in this instance only because it's being outweighed by the specific facts—trumped by them if you will.

We live our lives based on probabilities all the time anyway: Is it safe to drive home tonight, given the dangerous weather? Is this the very best medicine for this condition? What are the pros and cons of moving across the country? At many points, we all have major, potentially life-changing decisions to make.

Now there's this life-changing decision: Is Jesus Christ's message really true? Do we have enough evidence for his resurrection from the dead? Perhaps we are willing to conclude not just that these events probably happened, but that we should actually cry out, "Wow! He really was raised from the dead!" I think that we are there. I think this is what happened. The disciples witnessed the evidence upon evidence, what Luke calls "many convincing proofs" in Acts 1:3. So the question remains: are we ready to *commit ourselves* to Jesus Christ in light of his teachings—in effect, to say "I do" to him? Facts can make us inclined to decide something, but being sure is not the actual decision itself. After all, concluding that I should marry someone does not make me married!

Ankerberg: Next, a very important question for you personally. If you believe the historical facts about Jesus, does that make you a Christian? No. Well, then, what is faith? How does one become a Christian? Dr. Habermas answers these questions. Listen:

Habermas: Now, just about this time, I can picture an objection from the other side. Christians may be saying, "Whoa! This evidence is starting to look so good; what about faith? I mean, facts alone don't push or even get us into the Kingdom of God." But neither is faith a leap into the dark. In the New Testament, without exception, faith is based on trustworthy data. Paul said, back in 1 Corinthians 15:1-2, that when he came to Corinth, he preached the gospel message. On the factual side alone, definitions of the gospel in the New Testament include at least three truths. Present in the New Testament definition of the gospel are the Deity of Christ, his death, and his resurrection. Then Paul basically concluded here in this text, "If you believe these things, then you're saved. If not, then you are not."

In Christianity, there's always some content to saving belief. We call that the gospel data: the Deity, death, and the resurrection of Jesus Christ. But how does one move from the gospel data to salvation? Something is missing. The answer: facts plus faith equal salvation. But that's not quite accurate enough. In the New Testament, we do not place our faith in the historical facts per se, but we place our faith in Jesus, the person. I love history, but New Testament faith is not placed in history, it's placed in the Jesus Christ *of* history. Or, if you prefer, to get real exact here, the Jesus Christ of the gospel facts (his Deity, death, and resurrection) plus faith in him equals (leads to) one's salvation.

Faith is placed in the person of Jesus Christ. I've mentioned that it is sort of like marriage. I could be convinced that a woman is the best possible person on earth for me to marry. She's great here, she's wonderful there, and over here, too—everywhere, in fact. But you know what? If I don't say "I do," then we're not married. I think that's somewhat close to the New Testament picture. It's an analogy but a decent New Testament picture of what faith in Jesus Christ is. We could be convinced that Jesus did this and that he did that. He died for my sins, he was buried, and he rose again from the dead, too. He's even the Son of God. But according to the New Testament, if I don't say "I do" to him, if I refuse to say "I trust him," if I don't commit myself to him, then I'm not a Christian—just like I wouldn't be married without the equivalent. We're coming down now to what this means. The Jesus Christ of the gospel facts, plus faith, equals salvation. I think that's Paul's claim in the first two verses of 1 Corinthians 15:1-2.

Ankerberg: Gary Habermas said the facts plus faith equals salvation. Let me ask you, have you transferred your trust from yourself to Jesus for your salvation? The historical facts about Jesus are the foundation for anyone's faith-commitment to him. But the facts alone won't save you. Only the Jesus of the facts will save you. Each one who has ever become a Christian has realized via the facts that Jesus is real. But then they've experientially come to him in prayer and faith, telling him that they are sinners and transferring all of their trust to him. The Bible states that all men and women are separated from God because we have broken God's moral laws; we have sinned against him.

Second, the Bible says when Jesus was on the cross, our sins were placed on him, and he died in our place. He took the punishment that we deserve and could never repay and paid it in full. It's his gift to us. Now, if you will come to Jesus and admit you are a sinner and ask him to forgive you, he will do just that. You only need to say a prayer to him and entrust yourself into His hands. He will make you a Christian; he will forgive your sins and give you the gift of eternal life. The Bible says, "Whosoever shall call upon the name of the Lord shall be saved."[Acts 2:21] You say, "Don't I have to work for it? Don't I have to go to church first?" No. Eternal life is a gift. Paul says, "The wages of our sin is death, but the gift of God is eternal life through Jesus Christ our Lord." [Rom. 6:23] The Bible says God wants you to have his gift, the gift of eternal life, and there's nothing you can do to earn it. That's why it is a gift. And God will give you that gift the moment you place your trust in Jesus. All who have placed their trust in Jesus love him. It's out of our love for Jesus after we are saved that we want to serve him, but we don't serve him to get saved.

Now let me see if I can illustrate faith. Picture yourself on a two-story building. A fire starts on the first floor, and you rush up to the roof. There's no way to escape. The fire trucks come, and the firemen get out and bring a net. They look up at you, and they say, "Jump." You look down at the firemen and the net, and you say, "I can't. I'm afraid." The firemen say, "Don't you trust us? Don't you have faith?" You say, "Yeah, but it's two stories up." And they say, "Well, what choice do you have?" And you see the smoke and the flames coming up around you.

Now, just understanding the facts that those firemen can save you, will you be safe? No. Understanding facts won't save you. It's only when you step off of that building and you entrust yourself to those firemen and the net down below that you get saved. Some of you know the facts about Jesus, but you haven't entrusted yourself to him. You need to do that now.

But also, it's not the amount of faith that saves you. Let's say that you jumped off the building because you had faith, and now you get about halfway down, and you notice the firemen don't have a net, they're just holding hands. What good is your faith then? Will faith save you if you have placed it in the wrong object, namely, a group of firemen that can't save you? It's not your faith that saves you. You better make sure that you've got real firemen and a real net down there first.

In terms of salvation, it's not your faith that saves you but a real Jesus, who really did rise from the dead, the One who said that he was God and can forgive your sins and give you eternal life. He's the One you must place your faith in. Faith is really sticking your hand out to Jesus and saying, "I have nothing. Please give me your gift of eternal life." He promises He will.

Right now, would you pray and, by faith, place yourself into Jesus' hands and trust him to give you eternal life? You might say, "God, I know I'm a sinner. I know my sin has earned for me eternal separation from you. I believe Jesus died in my place when he died on the cross. I know that he rose again from the dead. I accept his death as the full payment for my sin. I accept him as my Savior. Thank you for saving me, in Jesus' name, I pray. Amen." If you prayed that prayer, the Bible says, "Whosoever shall call upon the name of the Lord shall be saved."

Others of you may be saying, "I just can't do that yet." If you delay trusting Christ for yourself, Dr. Habermas has this final word for you. Listen:

Habermas: Now, if you're sitting there wondering, "Look, I don't know. I'm a Hindu. I'm a Buddhist. I'm an agnostic. I'm an atheist." Sure, you can walk away and not believe in Jesus, but do you know what? I don't think you can walk away and say there's no data. I don't think you can walk away and say that there are no facts. I really wonder if you want to throw out or to ignore these facts because we can get to each one of them independently and for multiple reasons.

But do you know where all this is going? Paul says that it's because of the resurrection that death has no sting. It's because of the resurrection that the grave has no victory. Because of the resurrection of Jesus, we have the precious opportunity for eternal life. But we need to say "I do" to Jesus. It's all in whether we make that commitment. You know, you may believe someone wonderful is standing right next to you. Still, if you don't say "I do," you're not married. If you don't say "I do" to Jesus, what do you have? You still haven't trusted his teachings. "O death, where is your sting? O grave, where is your victory?" [1 Cor. 15:55] I leave you with the words of Jesus: "Because I live, ye shall live also." [John 14:19]

Further Resources

Liberty University Digital Commons links for Prof Gary R Habermas research, scholarship, and other relevant resources freely available:

http://bit.ly/1LGkYKq

General link to Liberty University Resources

http://digitalcommons.liberty.edu/

Prof Gary Habermas web site: "where everything is free":

www.garyhabermas.com

Dr. John Ankerberg web sites:

http://www.jashow.org/

https://www.youtube.com/user/johnankerberg

For permission to publish on websites, enquire of Prof Gary Habermas at

ghabermas@liberty.edu

Made in the USA
Las Vegas, NV
28 March 2021

20351918R00066